The House on
THIRD STREET

The Prequel to The Garbage Bag Girl

CAROL KNUTH

Dream Swept Publishing, LLC.

This book is a work of fiction, inspired by true events.
Most of the character names are fictional.

The House on Third Street. Copyright © 2015 by Carol Knuth

All rights reserved. No part of this publication may be reproduced or transmitted in any form without written permission from Dream Swept Publishing, LLC.

Dream Swept Publishing, LLC.
P.O. Box 18522
Erlanger, KY 41018

First paperback edition

ISBN: 0985924365

ISBN: 13: 9780985924362

Printed in the United States of America

For the three little girls

The House on
THIRD STREET

The Prequel to The Garbage Bag Girl

1

It was late, and as three-year-old Emma Snow looked at the two-story house, she yawned and rubbed her eyes. She and her family, her dad, Dean Snow, Dean's girlfriend, Maureen Dunford, and her two older sisters, six-year-old, Katie, and four-year-old, Amy, were standing on the sidewalk looking at their new house in Atlanta, Illinois.

Dean and Maureen had moved most of their belongings into the house earlier that day, before the heat of the summer afternoon set in. Now, almost Emma's bedtime, the three Snow girls were about to be taken on a tour of their new home. Emma's first impression of the house was that it was a towering, scary house of shadows.

Dean had just asked Emma what she thought of her new home, and was waiting for her response. Emma looked up at Dean and Maureen as they looked down at her. Emma did not want to go into the monster-sized white house with no lights glowing in its windows. At her young age, the two-story old house looked like a place where monsters lived.

Emma offered her dad and his girlfriend a small, strained smile. Satisfied with Emma's response, Dean turned away from Emma, and he and Maureen led the way up the narrow sidewalk to the wooden stairs they would use to gain access to the dark depths of the house.

Before Maureen was Dean's girlfriend, she had been just another of Emma's many babysitters. As a single parent, Dean was constantly on the lookout for someone to watch his daughters. In the last year, he had cycled through many babysitters of varying ages. He preferred his babysitters to be between 14 and 16 years old. Young girls were capable of watching kids, and they were more timid than older girls and women. When he put the moves on his teen babysitters, they were timid, caught off guard.

Maureen had been 18 when Dean met her, a little older than Dean would have liked for a babysitter, but still young enough to manipulate. Like many of the other girls that babysat for the Snow children, Dean had put the moves on Maureen. Most of the girls that babysat for the Snow girls did not last long because after Dean came onto them they were terrified and never babysat again, but Maureen was different. She stuck around, and eventually Dean accepted her as a long-term fixture in his life, as a live-in babysitter that also served a few of his other needs.

Emma's mother, Nancy, had abandoned Emma and her two older sisters, Katie, and Amy, over a year ago, when Emma was two years old. She had abandoned her children many times, leaving them for days at a time with strangers, and the last time she had not returned. After several days had passed, Dean had been contacted that he needed to come and pick up his children at which point, Dean became the sole custodian of Katie, Amy and Emma. Eventually, it was shared with Katie, Amy and Emma that their mother had passed away. No specifics were provided, just that their mother was dead.

Nancy had been a small woman with black hair, and a very loud voice. According to the conversations that Emma had overheard and from what Dean and Maureen had told her, Nancy had never wanted to be a mother. When she had found out that she was pregnant with her daughters, she tried to kill the babies by starving herself. Nancy had hoped, according to Dean, that if she didn't eat when she was pregnant then the baby would die while it was still inside of her, but she had failed in three fetus-killing attempts. She had hated being a mom, had felt trapped by the things that came with motherhood, like dirty diapers,

The House on Third Street

feeding babies, crying babies, and cuddling that babies needed. The crying had grated on Nancy's frazzled nerves, made more so by the pots of coffee she consumed throughout the day. Her answer to the stress of motherhood had been rope, and to chain smoke.

The noise her babies made, whether it was the sounds of her children laughing or crying, or the messes they made—their toys left unattended—were intolerable, and Nancy had found a solution. Rope was Nancy's babysitter. Instead of allowing Amy, three years old at the time, to mess up her house with toys, Nancy tied her to a chair. And to keep two-year-old Emma out of her hair, she isolated her in her bedroom, tied her up and left her in her bed for most of the day. She bound Emma's hands and feet so that she could not escape the bed, so that Nancy could drink her coffee and smoke her cigarettes, undisturbed.

Emma stayed close to her six-year-old sister, Katie, as she walked on the narrow sidewalk toward the house.

"Quit walking so close. Get away!" Katie said as she tried to peel her little sister's fingers from her arm.

Emma continued to press her slight form against her sister causing them both to walk in a shuffle together; it was that or they would fall in a tangle of little girl feet.

Dean and Maureen walked up the wooden steps, and then opened the old wooden door. As Emma watched, they stepped into the inky depths of the house. Emma was surrounded by darkness on the old, creaky porch as she tiptoed quietly, and closely, behind Katie. She clung to her sister's summer top, worrying the cotton between her fingers, willing Katie to walk faster, and hoping someone would turn on a light very soon.

Finally, Emma saw a glow of light ahead as she walked into the kitchen of her new home. She saw a table with shiny metal on its sides, a grey tabletop, and metal chairs pushed in around it on all four sides. There was a large, stained, white sink by another door. Emma looked up, way up, at the white metal mirror. What a strange place for a mirror, she considered. It was placed so very high. She thought that one day she would definitely have to pull a chair over to the sink, and then climb into the sink so she could see what was behind the hinged door of the mirror. Glancing across the room, she saw an old white refrigerator with rounded edges sitting next to the window, on the opposite wall.

Emma looked up at the ceiling, at the round light. It looked like a glowing doughnut flickering at her.

There was another door in the kitchen and Dean directed his three daughter's attention to it.

"Girls, come see our new bathroom," Dean said in his happy voice, a voice he did not use very often. He was standing by a funny looking door.

Dean grabbed the handle of the plastic accordion style bathroom door. The door looked like a fan when he opened and shut it. It had big jagged holes in it. Emma squatted on the floor on her hands and knees and peered up through the hole in the bottom of the door. She saw an old sink, shower, and a white toilet. She climbed to her feet and crowded into the small space with her sisters. Even pressing their three small bodies together, there was barely enough room for them in the small room.

"Stop touching me!" Katie said irritably.

Emma wrapped her arms around her shoulders, trying to make herself smaller, and stumbled into the toilet.

Dean walked away from the bathroom, continuing the tour of the house as Emma and her two older sisters, Katie and Amy, struggled to get out of the bathroom, each fighting to be the first one out of the tiny space.

Emma hurried to keep up with her sisters, not wanting to be left behind in any of the rooms, alone. She followed her sisters through the kitchen, and into what was to serve as the family's living room and noticed there were two more doors on the opposite wall of the room.

Emma looked around the living room, at the high ceiling, and at the shadows in the corners of the room. The floor was covered with old linoleum, with jagged pieces missing from it. It was black and light grey, and had what looked like a red floral design. It was faded by the many feet that had crossed its surface, and faded by time. There was an old brown metal object standing in one corner of the room.

Dean saw his daughters looking at the brown object and walked toward it.

"It's a furnace," he said, grinning. "It'll keep the downstairs warm in the winter."

They did not need it now, Emma thought, because the summer heat outside was lingering in the house.

Emma looked at the big round wooden table with swirly legs holding it up, placed in the center of the room, her head just reaching the top of the table's surface.

"What do you think?" Maureen asked. "My mommy let me bring her special table to our new house."

Emma looked around at the rest of the room and saw there was a comfortable looking couch resting against the wall, a tall black rocking chair nearby, and a small brown table positioned between the two. It was all so different, the house and the furniture.

Maureen sat in the black rocking chair, gently swaying back and forth, as she stroked its arm.

Maureen shared that she had found the pretty couch at a store, on sale. She looked very happy as she looked at her brown table, rocking chair, and her pretty couch. To Emma it was a big scary house, but Maureen and her daddy did not seem to find the house scary at all.

Dean opened one of the doors at the far end of the room and turned to look down at each of his blonde-haired little girls.

In a very serious, deep voice, Dean said that the room was his bedroom, his and Maureen's bedroom. He flipped the light switch dispelling the darkness. Katie, Amy, and Emma scooted into the room and stood beside a bed that was positioned against the one wall of the room with no windows. This was to be Dean's special space, so she held her hands in front of her tight so she would not be tempted to touch anything and make him mad at her. She could not wait until it was time to leave this brightly lit room. She did not want to be in her daddy's bedroom with his big bed sitting in the middle of the room.

The light in this room was brighter; no shadows reached the corners. It was a funny room. It looked almost like a circle—a circle room—but the walls were flat, with lots of windows. Dean instructed his daughters that they were *not* allowed in his room without his permission. Then he placed his finger on the light switch and Emma knew the tour of his special room was over. The switch made a loud clicking noise, and then the room was bathed in darkness. Dean closed the door behind them and then walked over to the other door in the living room and opened it.

Emma saw a dark hall with two doors on the left side, and when she looked straight ahead, there were two big black doors. She walked behind her sisters as they followed Dean and Maureen down the hall and around the corner to the foot of the stairs. Emma walked as close to her sisters as possible, shuffling her feet in tiny steps so she would not trample her sisters with the tips of her shoes.

The possibility existed that Katie or Amy might smack her, Emma thought, if she got too close to them, but that was just a chance she would have to take. The alternative of having something scary reach out from behind her—whatever monster was lurking in the shadows waiting to steal her away—well, she just could not let that happen. She would just have to stick as close to her sisters as possible. Chances were that a monster would not try to capture her, she reasoned, if it saw that she was not alone, or maybe the monster would not be able to see very well in the dark hallway. When the monster looked at Emma's sisters and her, she hoped it would think they were one big person instead of three little girls and her the smallest one of all.

The dark brown door closed behind them and Emma could only move forward to see what was up ahead. As they walked down the corridor, Emma looked up, way up into the darkness. It was so dark, and the ceiling was so high that she could not see what was waiting for her.

The stairs seemed to fade away into the dark depths of nothingness. Emma was the last one in line, the last to walk around the corner in the hall, walking past the big black double doors. She had to stop for a minute, while her family slowly crawled up the stairs. Pausing for a minute, she reached her hand up toward the thick, swirly railing, not quite tall enough to reach it, and propped her foot on the first worn wooden step. She looked behind her at the two tall black doors with the big windows that framed the darkness outside. Her heart skipped a beat as she imagined a face pressed against the smudged dark window, watching her. Pressing her face into Amy's back, Emma tried to help her up the stairs, quickly, as she struggled to be free of the dark hallway and potential dangers that lay within.

Dean had flicked on the light switch that was just out of Emma's reach on the wall, by the door when they had entered the hallway. It felt to Emma as if she were in a pretend cave, something out of a scary fairy tale, or like when she hid beneath her blankets at night when she was scared, which was most nights. It was creepy dark in the hall, and now, as she moved forward, ever so slowly up the stairs, the darkness pressed in on her.

Finally, Emma made it to the top of the stairs. Dean, Maureen and her sisters were all standing on the landing waiting for her. Emma could see the faint outline of another hallway wrapping around in kind of a circle that disappeared down yet another hallway. But Dean was not going down the hallway into the dark; he was standing in front of the door at the top of the steps. He had his hand on the doorknob looking down at his children.

"Okay, girls, are yuh ready to see your room?" Dean asked, excitedly.

It seemed to Emma that her new bedroom was in a far off dark place, away from the rest of the house. Dean opened the door to the room, and all Emma could see was more black, no shapes could be seen.

Emma was still peering into the dark room, trying to make out the contents of the room when suddenly there was a brilliant flash of white light. Speckles of color danced in Emma's eyes due to the unexpected burst of light in the room. Brightly lit, this room was not dark and dim like the rest of the house. There were no shadows to be found in the corners, either. Swinging and bobbing, making a tinkling sound as the metal beaded chain hit the glass, a light bulb swung freely from a wire from the high ceiling. Dean explained that the girls were to pull the string to turn on the light because there was no light switch on the wall.

Although there were no shadows in the room, the room still scared Emma. As she stood in the center of the bedroom, she noticed that there was a second door in the room. Not the door she had come through, but a second one with a hook-latch on it.

Dean walked across the room, flipped up the hook-latch, and pushed the door open. He swung his arm around his head as he walked into the black room. Click and flash went the light bulb that hung from the ceiling in the strange new room filled with all kinds of things. Clothes were hung on a metal rod on one side of the room, and wooden chairs were stacked on the other side. A strange black box with a glass eye in its center with a cloth hanging off it was in the far corner. Dean said the black box was not a box at all; it was a really old camera. There was a big black treasure trunk in the room, too. The room was filled with the treasures the previous owners of the house had owned. The room was crammed full, with barely any room to stand.

Dean shared that the old people that used to live in the house had left lots of their things behind and they were stored in the room. He instructed his daughters not to touch anything in the room and not to play in the room.

He did not have to worry about Emma playing in the creepy room. She hoped the room would always be shut tight and locked.

Dean walked back into the attached room that was to become the three little girl's bedroom. There were two big beds placed next to each other on either side of the room, with a window in between. Emma stood at the foot of the beds as Dean shared the story of the old people that used to live in the house.

"How you girls like your new beds?" Dean asked as he propped his hands on his hips. Not waiting for a response, he said, "Yuh know, there used to be an old lady and an old man that lived in this house. A long time ago," Dean paused for effect, "they had a farm outside of town. When they got too old to farm, they had their house moved into town, and they lived here until they died."

Wide-eyed, Emma looked up at Dean.

"They died in these very beds," Dean said, no longer smiling.

Horrified, Emma forgot to breathe for a minute. She stood at the foot of one of the beds and pictured an old woman dressed in a frilly white nightgown buttoned to her chin, her eyes closed tight as she choked on her last breath.

Dean had decided that Amy and Katie would sleep in the big bed to the right of the window and Emma would sleep in the other bed. It was the same size as the other bed, big enough for two adults.

Emma looked from one bed to the other, noticing how different they were. Amy and Katie's bed had gray metal bars for a headboard and the other bed had a really high, shiny dark and light mixed colored headboard. She knew if she stood up, the headboard would be taller than she was. The beds did not match, and were monstrously big for a little girl to sleep in.

The room felt all wrong, and looked wrong to Emma. It was all wrong. Emma thought how scary it was going to be to sleep all alone in the very big, un-matching bed where old people had died. She looked around at the rest of the room and saw two brown wooden dressers, probably belonging to the dead people.

Dean called the girls over to a corner of the room, showing them a brown metal grate on the floor. It was pretty with all the swirls twirling this way and that, kind of like a garden filled with wild flowers. He demonstrated how to slide the bar on the side to open it. Dean explained that during winter, they could open it, and that was how heat would get into their bedroom. Katie, Amy and Emma knelt down, huddling on the floor around the metal grate, and opened it to see the floor and room below.

"Time for bed," Dean said from behind the girls.

Maureen had gone downstairs while the three little girls had been looking through the grate. When Emma looked up from where she was sitting on the floor, she saw that Maureen was holding nightgowns in her hands.

"Emma, here's your nightgown," Maureen said in a tired voice.

Emma climbed to her feet and walked over to Maureen, reaching for the gown.

Once the girls were jammied up, Dean boomed, "Time to get in bed!"

That was it. Emma panicked knowing the lights would be turned off soon, leaving her in the darkness. She grabbed at the blanket on the big bed for leverage and climbed up. Katie and Amy were already lying beneath their blankets snuggled together in bed. Emma slid under her blanket and lay her head on the old flat pillow that smelled like wet dog. She turned on her side so she could see her sisters.

"Good night, girls," Maureen said as she walked over to the swinging light. She yanked the string, and click, the world became black.

Emma felt panicky. Her heart began to flutter. She could not see her sisters in their bed anymore. It was too dark. Emma felt like she was all alone in the unfamiliar room. Scared, she flipped the blanket up over her head in a room already too warm. Her hot breath made it even hotter under the blanket. Emma's heart raced as she listened to all the noises of the strange old house.

2

The bedroom Emma shared with her two older sisters was dark. Days earlier, Maureen had covered the windows with a towel because of the agonizingly painful headaches the little girls had. There was not a part of Emma's body that did not hurt. She felt weak and tired, barely able to lift her arms and legs from the bed. Her light blonde hair clung to her face, damp with sweat from fever. Emma was lying curled on her side with her eyes closed tight wishing the pain in her stomach and head would go away.

Katie and Amy were lying in misery on their bed, nearby. The three little girls were sick with both chicken pox and measles, burning up with fevers, and itchy with oozing sores. Every inch of their bodies ached. Over the past week, Emma's fever had climbed steadily, and now the fever rested at a dangerously high level, but still Dean refused to take her to see a doctor.

Emma wished Maureen were home, but she had left for work, leaving her home with Dean. All of a sudden, Emma got that feeling, that mouth-watering, queasy feeling. She pressed her hands against her stomach, and squeezed her eyes shut tighter. She was exhausted, her body felt heavy; she could barely make her body move. She opened one eye just a peep as her stomach did another flip. The room spun dizzily as she pushed herself up and tried to scoot her bottom to the side of the bed, trying to make it to the metal bucket Dean had placed in the center of the room.

Vomit exploded from Emma, all over the sheet, pillow and blanket. The sticky smelly goo was in her hair and had splashed onto the wall beside the bed.

"Daddy! Daddy! Emma threw up," Katie cried, weakly.

Emma heard Dean's boots pounding on the wooden steps in the hall. It sounded to Emma as if his big feet were pounding inside her head. The pain was nauseating, and she threw up again. Emma's heart thudded and her head spun dizzily. She saw the outline of Dean's body in the doorway, and watched as he walked across the room. Emma looked up into his face when he stopped at the side of her bed, and saw the fury on his face. For a moment, he just stood there, his hands on his blue jeaned hips, looking at the vomit on the bed, and on Emma. His head tilted up as he noticed the newly vomit stained wall. Emma shuddered.

She wrapped her arms around her legs, tight, to steel herself from what she knew was sure to come, Dean's fists. The cold November air chilled her exposed legs. Vomit was matted in her hair and the smell made her stomach roll.

Dean took a step toward his youngest child.

Vomit exploded from her—all over the bed and spattered the front of his jeans.

"Son of a bitch," Dean shouted. Slowly he looked down at his jeans.

"What the—Emma, can't you get the fuck out of the Goddamn bed. You had to puke *all* over. *Bitch*. Now I have tuh clean this fuckin' shit up."

Dean clenched his hands into fists.

Emma watched as Dean, as if in slow motion, pulled one of his arms back, and then watched as his fist came toward her with dizzying speed, smashing into the side of her face. She tumbled over onto her side, landing in a pool of vomit. She felt his fists hitting her body, and then felt her body being picked up, felt the freedom of air as she left his hands, and then met the hard wall with her head, face, shoulder and hip. She fell back onto the bed as Dean grabbed her small head, holding tightly to her long hair for leverage, and slammed her head into the wall. She went limp as she blacked out.

After almost 24 hours had passed, Dean became scared that his youngest daughter, Emma, was not going to wake up. He walked across the lawn to his mother's house, and asked what he should do about Emma.

Harriet, his mother, followed Dean back to his house; stood next to Emma's bed and looked down at her; stared at her unconscious granddaughter. She advised Dean that he needed to take Emma to the hospital immediately because it looked to her as if she was dying.

Dean shared that he was concerned that a doctor would recognize that Emma was not just a very sick little girl, but that her unconscious state had something to do with the bruises on her body. He argued against taking her to the hospital.

"I have a doctor friend in town that I've gotten friendly with. Take her to him," Harriet insisted.

"Will he see her today? She's not even one of his patients," Dean whined. He worried what would happen if Emma died, if the police thought he was responsible for her death.

"Oh, he'll see 'er. He will if he doesn't want his wife to find out he's been screwing me," Harriet sneered.

Harriet called her doctor friend, and later that day, Dean took Emma to his office where she was examined.

When the doctor examined Emma, he noticed the bruises on her body, but knew to keep his mouth shut about them. Aside from the obvious signs of physical abuse, she was a very sick little girl. She was stirring, the doctor noticed, awake now, which was a very good sign, but she was dehydrated and still feverish, and the right side of her face was paralyzed caused possibly by the beating that he suspected she had received. Admitting her into the hospital for a few days was the care that she needed, he explained to Dean. Dean, however, refused to check his daughter into the hospital, instead he insisted that he could care for her at his home.

Knowing that there was nothing more that he could do for Emma, the doctor shared with Dean that the right side of Emma's face was paralyzed. Her right eye would not close, so it needed to be covered with a patch until she recovered the use of her facial muscles. The doctor gave Dean eye drops and told him that it was important to place drops, which would act as tears for her eye, into her eye several times a day to keep her eye moist. He also shared that the facial paralysis should subside with time, and that it was important to help her exercise her facial muscles to decrease long-term damage.

The doctor gave Emma a few tablets to get her fever down, which she washed down with a small paper cup of water. He then instructed Dean to watch her fever, and that if it spiked, to give her one of the pills from the bottle he handed to him. She needs rest, lots of rest, the doctor shared. The doctor's last words of advice for Dean was that if her symptoms worsened, if she fell asleep and did not wake up, then he must take her to the emergency room.

Dean had no intention of taking his daughter to the emergency room. On the drive home, Dean said, "Get better, Emma. I don't have time to be driving you all over the place, and money don't grow on trees."

Emma was awake, lying on the backseat of the car. She had heard Dean's voice, but she did not respond.

"And stop doing stupid things to make me mad," Dean mumbled.

Twenty minutes later, when they arrived at the house on Third Street, relieved that he had dodged the potential murder charge bullet, Dean handed Emma off to Maureen and told her to put drops in her eye several times a day, and shared that she was going to be fine.

It was a struggle to get the muscles in Emma's face and tongue to cooperate, to work as they had before Dean had beaten her causing her paralysis. Emma seemed to be at war with her face, she willing it to work as it had before, and it protesting. But gradually, Emma was able to close and open her eye and move her tongue and lips. She continued to have difficulty speaking without slurring her words. She began to hate words that started with the *s* sound, like soup, and little girls named Sally. Eating was a chore as food and liquid dribbled down her chin when she worked hard to eat like the big girl she knew she was.

Emma knew her family watched her, stared at her new face. Maureen explained to Emma that now she was like the little duck in the book. Emma flipped through the pages of the book that Maureen had given her, looked at the ugly bird and the white bird it became. She didn't really understand the story, and didn't think the duck was ugly, but knew that the other birds thought it was ugly, just as other people thought she had become an ugly little girl because her face didn't work right anymore.

She was an ugly little girl, Emma thought.

Within a few months, Emma was feeling much better, aside from the droopy eye and lisp. Life in the house on Third Street continued on as usual, with a great deal of shouting and fighting between Maureen and Dean.

As the months passed, the arguments and fights between Maureen and Dean became increasingly violent. After many black eyes and broken bones, a pregnant Maureen packed her personal belongings and left, moving in with Dean's sister, Marjorie. Without a babysitter to take on the responsibility of his children, Dean gave the state custody of seven-year-old Katie, five-year-old Amy and an almost four-year-old Emma.

It was a simple process, giving ones children to the state where one lived. Dean's mother found the information Dean needed to do just that, and one February afternoon, per the states agreement, Dean drove his children to a foster home two hours south from where his home was located. The three girl's foster mother, Mrs. Pugsley, was elderly, in her sixties, and to make the situation seem more natural to the children, Dean and Mrs. Pugsley decided the children should call her Grandma.

Grandma turned toward Katie, Amy and Emma, and opening her arms wide, smiled and said, "Hi girls! I'm so happy to see you."

The stranger looked down at the three little girls and proceeded to say hello to them, saying their names as if she was their real grandmother and had known them for years, instead of the reality, having just met them.

The three little girls were very quiet as they looked up at the woman.

Emma was happy to meet the new grandma. Meeting strangers was one of the most familiar things to her, having been passed from stranger's home to stranger's home since she was born. Consistency was the stranger to Emma, not change, and certainly not strangers.

Since Maureen had left Dean, there was no one to keep his rage in check. Emma was singled out by her father, receiving the brunt of his anger, his yelling, and blows by his fists. Yes, she was very happy to be handed over to this new stranger, if it meant Dean would no longer hit her.

Grandma invited Dean and his daughters into the house, and she took them on a tour, showing them her brightly lit kitchen, cozy living room and the bedroom they would share during their stay. The three children and two adults became acquainted over cups of coffee for the adults, and milk for the girls, in the kitchen. When Dean's cup was empty, he exited the kitchen and drove away, back to his house on Third Street.

As the weeks passed, Emma found that she liked staying with her newest grandma and grandma's two dogs. Grandma didn't yell at Katie, Amy and Emma when they laughed and played, or when they sang. Her house was always clean; she had toys for Emma and her sisters to play with, and everything was always in the same place. And she did not yell or hit the three little girls when they forgot to put their toys away, instead, she explained that when they were done playing with the toys, they were to put the toys back where they had gotten them. Everything had a place where it belonged, she explained, even toys. At Dean's house, Emma could never find anything. There were no special places for things, and sometimes Dean, when he was in one his dark moods, would snatch up all their toys and throw them away.

Every day, Grandma made sure the girls had something good to eat, and they ate their meals in the bright, cozy kitchen. The room had a big window, a pretty frilly curtain hanging from the top of the window, and there was a table in the room, covered by a tablecloth. There was a door with a window with a matching frilly curtain, in the room that led to the outside. Emma could see the sky and the trees when she looked out of the windows.

When Grandma worked in the kitchen—cooking and baking—her little dogs would scamper underfoot. Grandma loved her two small dogs, and she treated them as if they were her children.

One morning, after Katie and Amy had left for school on the bus, Grandma took Emma to the garage and showed her the *special* shelf, where she kept the dog things. Then Grandma showed Emma how to brush the dogs with a brush that looked like it was for little girls.

"Emma, come here, honey," Grandma said. "I want to show you something."

Grandma opened the garage door and walked toward a workbench. Emma followed her to see what surprise she might have for her.

"Sweetie, this is where I keep the brushes for my dogs. They love to be brushed. Here, I'll show you," Grandma said as she knelt down next to the dogs.

Emma squatted down near Grandma and the dogs, and watched as the furry creatures jumped and barked in excitement. Grandma began pulling the brush gently through the smaller dog's fur. The dog became calm and sat quietly.

"Here you go," Grandma said in a coaxing tone. "Now you try it. Don't be afraid. They'll be your friends if you brush them. Look how he's wagging his tail. That means he's your friend."

Emma looked up at Grandma's smiling face and returned her smile. She accepted the dog brush in her small hand, and did her very best to brush the smaller dog as she had been shown. Grandma was right she thought with a smile, the dog was wagging its tail. He must like me, she thought, gaining confidence in her task. She wanted the dogs to be her friends so they wouldn't bite her. She knew dogs could be mean and bite, because Dean had had dogs that were mean, dogs that had tried to bite her. After that day, when her sisters were at school, Emma would spend time with her new furry friends, brushing their coats until smooth.

Each evening, Katie, Amy, Emma and Grandma would have supper together, and Katie and Amy would share stories about their day at school. Some evenings, Grandma's daughter and her family would visit for a few hours. Other times, Grandma's friend, the social worker, would come over to the house to visit. The social worker was a very nice lady and liked to talk about things that Emma did not really understand so she just smiled and showed her pictures she had colored.

On Sunday mornings, Emma went to school, too. She attended the local Christian church with Grandma, Katie and Amy. It was in that little classroom that Emma's teacher taught her about God. The teacher told her that God would always be with her, even when people were bad to her, and He loved her very much.

Emma loved when spring arrived at Grandma's house, loved the warm feeling of the sun on her skin, loved watching the green leaves as they blew in the breeze, and loved watching the butterflies flit about seemingly in no hurry to be anywhere. She especially loved her afternoon walks with Grandma before her sisters arrived home on the big school bus.

No cars ever drove by on the old country road so it was okay to stop and watch the occasional fluffy cloud family, which they did often. Their walks were never rushed, plenty of time for Grandma to point out the cloud people and cloud animals in the sky. Grandma had the patience and appreciation for the simple things that come with advanced years, and shared this gift with Emma.

Grandma would get down on one knee, close to Emma, drape her arm around her waist, and point to the white fluffy clouds in the blue sky.

"Do you see that cloud there in the sky, that one right there?" Grandma asked.

Emma squinted up at the sky, shielding her eyes with her small hands, almost as if she were looking through a pair of binoculars.

"Uh-huh," Emma answered.

"It's a little girl floating in the sky," Grandma said softly.

As they continued their walk, Emma kicked her little tennis shoes at the dusty dirt road making little dirt smokes fly in the air away from her. She heard the birds singing as they walked down the country road as the breeze lifted her blonde hair behind her.

Sometimes their walks would take them to the gas station at the edge of town, and Emma knew it meant a pop out of the pop machine. When they arrived at the gas station, they would walk through the open door as Grandma said 'good afternoon' to the attendant, and then they walked straight to the pop machine sitting against the wall in the hall by the door. Emma liked the way the yellow glow of the lights shined on the assortment of pop bottles of various flavors. Grandma would slide the change, change that she had slid into her pocket before they had left the house for their walk, into the money slot and let Emma choose the flavor of pop she wanted.

"What kind of pop would you like today, honey?" Grandma asked.

"Mmmm," Emma pondered, pressing a finger to her lips. Deep in thought, she considered which flavor of pop she should choose, as if it were a very important decision she was making. Grandma waited patiently.

After Emma made her selection, Grandma opened the glass door and tugged the small glass bottle out of its position and then placed the bottle under the cap remover and popped off the top, then handed the bottle to Emma.

Emma liked the way the pop tickled her nose as she sniffed in the flavor of the day, either purple or orange.

Emma and her sisters slept in the same bedroom at their foster grandma's house. All the toys she had given them, and their clothes, fit in the bedroom, even with two beds and a dresser in the room. It was a pretty room. Everything matched; the bedspreads were the same, and it even had curtains on the windows, and they matched, too. At the end of the day, after Emma and her two sisters were snuggled in their beds, Grandma would sit down on one of the beds and have the little girls say their nighttime prayer together.

"Now I lay me down to sleep...," they said in a chorus.

After Grandma tucked in Katie and Amy, she walked over to Emma's bed, leaned over and made sure the blanket was snuggly around the little Snow girl. She smoothed Emma's hair off her face.

Lying on her side, Emma watched Grandma walk to the door leading to the hall.

Grandma turned back toward the room, and the girls, and gave them one last smile for the day.

"Goodnight, girls. Sleep tight," Grandma said, gently.

"Goodnight, Grandma," the girls chorused sweetly, and sleepily.

Grandma left the door open a crack so the girls could see the light from the TV she would be watching in the living room as they drifted off to sleep.

4

One summer evening, after supper, Katie, Amy, and Emma were playing in the living room while Grandma sat in her favorite chair nearby, reading her newspaper. The lamp on the table next to her chair created a soft glow on her paper and her face. Occasionally, Emma took a break from playing and glanced over at Grandma, just to make sure she was still there. It was an evening like many others they had shared, but Emma had a bad feeling, the feeling she had frequently when she had lived with Dean.

She sighed a little girl sigh and turned back to her crayons and coloring book. She chose a crayon with care, removing it from its place in the Indian headdress crayon holder. She wanted just the right colors for her picture.

Her head snapped up when she heard a knock on the front door, and she watched Grandma as she rose from her chair and walked to the door, and then opened it.

There standing in the doorway was Dean and Maureen. Maureen was holding what looked like a little doll in a white blanket.

In an instant, the quiet cozy evening was over.

What is Dean doing here, Emma worried? He was probably just visiting, she considered, trying to reassuring herself. She was not happy to have her evening of quiet coloring with Grandma interrupted.

Grandma, Dean, and Maureen stood by the door, talking for a few minutes. Emma watched them, trying to hear what they were saying. Katie and Amy were watching them, too.

Grandma turned away from Dean and Maureen, and walked over to the little girls. "Girls, your daddy and Maureen have come to take you home with them," Grandma said.

Emma looked at Dean and then at Grandma, confused. This was her home now, she thought. She didn't want to go back to the house on Third Street with Dean and Maureen, back to his yelling and hitting.

Katie and Amy sat quietly at the table and stared at Dean and Maureen.

Emma scrambled out of her chair and ran into the other room, the room with the piano, hoping she could hide and no one would find her. She wanted Dean and Maureen to leave without her. *They had other little girls. They didn't need her.* She belonged to Grandma now, not Dean, she thought, stubbornly.

Grandma walked into the dark room, looking for Emma. It didn't take long to find her hiding place. Kneeling down beside the little girl, gently Grandma swept the stray strands of hair away from Emma's face.

Emma stared at the carpeted floor. She thought if she didn't look up, then Grandma couldn't tell her that she had to go with Dean.

Grandma sat down next to Emma. "Emma, you have a new mommy. Maureen and your daddy got married. It will be wonderful to have a new mommy." Grandma picked up Emma's small hand and held it in her bigger hand. She patted Emma's small fragile hand.

Emma scooted closer to Grandma, and lay her head against her body, trying to absorb the safeness that she provided, and represented. She knew Dean had come to take her sisters and her away with him, away from peace, quiet, and safety.

"Are you ready?" Grandma asked as she looked down into Emma's green eyes.

Emma felt so sad, felt tears burning her eyes. *Jesus, please save me from my daddy. Please, please don't make me go with him, back to all the bad things.*

Grandma stood up and held out her hand to Emma.

Emma placed her hand in Grandma's hand, and let her pull her to her feet. Emma held tightly to Grandma's hand, pulling it to her cheek.

"Please, Grandma," Emma said, softly. "Don't make me go. I'll be good. Please let me stay. I won't be bad. I promise."

Grandma placed her free hand against Emma's cheek, and said, sadly, "Oh, honey, I know you're a good girl. I wish you could stay with me longer, but it's time for you to go back home with your daddy. He's missed you so much and wants you to come home with him. It'll be okay. Everything's going to be okay."

Still, Emma did not release her hand.

"Emma," Grandma said, softly, "would you like to take some of your toys home with you? Would you like to take your crayons and the Indian headdress to hold your crayons? You can take the harmonica with you, too. That way you can practice your beautiful music. I bet your daddy would love to hear you play music for him."

Grandma smiled at Emma. "I know, let's go show your daddy the snake that jumps out of the can. It'll be so funny when he's surprised by the snake." Grandma tugged gently at Emma's hand, coaxing her into the other room where Dean was waiting.

Emma held Grandma's hand as she collected the toys for her to take to Dean's home.

Standing in the doorway of the living room, Emma looked at Dean, Maureen, and the baby perched on Grandma's couch.

"Emma," Grandma said in feigned cheerfulness, "show your daddy your harmonica."

Hesitantly, Emma raised the shiny silver harmonica to her lips and blew softly into the holes, barely enough air to create a sound.

"That sure is a pretty harmonica, Emma," Dean said with false enthusiasm.

Emma looked around the room and panicked when she realized Grandma had left her alone with Dean and Maureen.

"Here we are," Grandma said cheerfully, when moments later, she walked back into the room. She had Katie, Amy and Emma's little suitcase in her hand.

Emma lowered the harmonica in fear and defeat. She wasn't going to stay with Grandma. God wasn't going to save her today. She had to go home with Dean. Emma felt a heavy weight of sadness on her shoulders. It felt as if Dean were sitting on her, holding her down as he sometimes did when he was playing, except it usually made her cry because she couldn't breathe and he wouldn't let her up.

Emma slowly looked from Maureen's face, to Dean's face, to Grandma's face. She knew the adults expected her sisters and her to put on their happiest faces. The children were supposed to be happy to be going home with Dean and on to their next scary adventure. But Emma didn't want to put on her happy face. She didn't want to pretend to be happy. She didn't want to leave her safe, clean, happy home with Grandma. She didn't want to go home with angry Dean. She didn't want to move again. She wanted to stay right here, never packing her little suitcase, ever again, never again wondering where she would wake up.

Grandma walked over to Emma and knelt down in front of her. She reached for her hands and held them, calming her. "Honey, you be a good girl. I love you," Grandma said, softly.

Sadly, Emma looked into Grandma's eyes, not wanting to leave her but knowing she had to. "Okay," Emma whispered.

Grandma wrapped her arms around Emma, gave her one last hug, and whispered in her ear, "I love you, and Jesus will watch over you."

Emma whispered, "I love you, too."

When she pulled back, Emma could see that Grandma's eyes were all watery, just like hers were. After Grandma placed the silver harmonica, the snake that jumped out of its can and the Indian headdress filled with crayons into a bag and handed it to Emma, Emma walked toward the door. Emma looked back at the living room, at the small table where she had colored in coloring books after dinner each evening, and she looked at the comfortable chair that sat by the fireplace where Grandma sat watching TV. Emma looked into the kitchen, dark now, dinner long since over, barely able to make out the shapes of the table and chairs. She glanced down the hall where her bedroom had been for the past several months, and lastly, she looked up into Grandma's face. Such sadness, Emma thought that surely her heart would burst.

The three little girls said their goodbyes to Grandma, not realizing that after they walked across the threshold, and were driven away, down the long driveway, they would never see their foster grandma again.

As Emma walked out Grandma's door for the last time, she hoped Dean wouldn't be mad at her anymore, wouldn't hurt her. Now that he and Maureen were married, and she was going to live with them all the time, she hoped Dean would be happy. Maybe it would be okay, Emma hoped. Maybe Dean wouldn't hurt her like last time.

Emma climbed into the car, and as she scooted onto the seat, she hoped that the Jesus that Grandma and her Sunday school teacher had told her about really would go with her to Dean's house and protect her, just in case Dean got mad again.

5

School would begin in a few weeks, and Emma was excited to be starting Kindergarten. Katie would be in 3rd grade and Amy in 1st grade. Emma was excited to start school for several reasons, one of which was to escape from the house on Third Street, for a few hours each day, and starting Kindergarten meant she was growing up, just like her sisters.

Each night, after showers were taken, Maureen picked out the dresses Katie, Amy and Emma would wear the next day to school, writing their names on little pieces of paper and then pinning them to each dress. Then the next morning, after Maureen had left for work, and the babysitter helped the girls prepare for their day at school, they would know which dress to wear.

Katie and Amy attended school in the brick school building across town, where 1st through 12th graders attended, and Emma attended Kindergarten a block from the family home. Emma walked to and from school by herself each day. She wasn't afraid of walking to school by herself, knowing the bad and scary things only happened at her house, knew her family was different, that Dean was different from other dad's. Emma tried to remember how it felt not to be afraid or sad. She prayed each night, just like her foster grandma taught her, and believed, just like her Sunday school teacher and Grandma had taught her, that Jesus loved her and was watching over her.

The Kindergarten teacher reminded Emma of her foster grandma because she was kind and patient, but she was much younger. Emma was always on her best behavior at school, wanting her teacher to be proud of her and praise her.

Her teacher would bend down toward her, and look into Emma's eyes, and smile.

"Emma, sweetie, super job," the teacher would say.

Besides art, Emma's favorite part of the day was story time. The teacher would gather all the children in class, instructing them to sit in a half-circle near her while she read to them. There would be a hush in the room, not even a whisper as the children listened attentively. As the teacher read the stories, Emma could imagine being the little goat that pranced across the bridge with the other goats and could imagine skipping in the forest with the little girl wearing the red cape to visit her grandma. She couldn't wait until the day she could read to herself, and then she could go on adventures, go to all of the places in the books that she read with all the interesting people.

Each day, when the teacher announced that the school day was over, Emma was always the last child to walk out of the classroom, never ready to go home. The house on Third Street was filled with shouting and hitting, and often it was directed at her. Maureen and Dean had bad days, and when they had a bad day, it meant Emma would have a *very* bad day. Emma was shaken, beaten with a belt, a switch, or yardstick, so she didn't want to go home.

Emma was hot under the sheet. Sweat created a path down her forehead, and the back of her neck. But as hot as she was, she pulled the sheet tighter over her head and rolled onto her side trying to block out the sounds of the footsteps. Terrified, she held her breath and listened, trying to hear the ghost footsteps to determine if they were coming closer. Panting because she was swelteringly hot and because she was afraid, Emma wondered if it was coming for her, whatever or whoever belonged to the sound of footsteps. Her heart raced and she thought surely it would burst in her little chest, and she strained her good ear to hear. She was burning up. She wished she were a braver little girl so she could walk to the kitchen for a cup of water, but that was out of the question because of the danger in the house at night, from the footsteps and from Maureen and Dean. She pulled the sheet tighter, her entire body sealed inside as if in a cocoon. The footsteps didn't sound as if they were closer, she decided, but they didn't sound as if they were going farther away either.

The sound of the footsteps had begun almost as soon as they had moved into the house, the steps sounding as if they were far away at first then coming closer and closer. She knew the sound of Dean's work boots on the wooden floor in the hall and on the stairs, and that was what it sounded like, like his footsteps.

Dean had shared with Katie, Amy and Emma that people had died in the house, and the three little girls had talked about the ghosts, and decided that surely they lived in the house with them. They didn't think they were angry, or bad ghosts. They were just the spirits of those who had once lived in the home and for some reason had chosen not to abandon the house. Emma thought that maybe it was the ghosts she heard roaming the halls of the house, and it was to that thought that she fell asleep. As she dozed, the sound of footsteps stopped. A floorboard creaked. The footsteps resumed, becoming fainter as they walked away from the sleeping five-year-old little girl.

6

By the time Emma was in third grade, she had become quite the connoisseur of beatings. Her stepmother's beatings were just as painful and embarrassing as Dean's were, however she didn't use a belt or a switch from the tree in front of the house. Another difference was that Maureen didn't insist that Emma pull her pants down to her ankles, but she *would* have Katie and Amy watch the beatings, just as Dean did.

During some of the beatings, Emma would be instructed to stand, then either Dean or Maureen would grasp her upper arm, and depending on the beater, she would be beaten with a spoon, yardstick, belt or stick. She supposed if she had to choose between the object used to beat her, she preferred the yardstick. Her stepmother was much more creative in her beatings and forms of punishments. Maureen would get a tight grip on Emma's arm, then when she was ready to proceed, she would whale away with the yardstick, hitting Emma with all her might, over and over again, until her arm wore out.

It was always the worst to be beaten in the summer when Emma was wearing one of her little dresses or shorts. It was embarrassing to let the neighborhood kids see the purple and black bruises on the back of her legs. It hurt more, too, since the wood from the stick hit her tender skin and not through her pants. One time she had been instructed to lay on the floor as her sisters knelt down on their knees in front of her, and she was beaten with a broken yardstick. Lying on the floor during a beating was even worse than standing. At least when she was standing, her body could flinch and writhe from each blow. When she had to lie still on her stomach with her arms above her head and her legs straight back behind her, her body was unable to contort with the pain, unable to move. Being unable to move or flinch was a new horrible form of torture, even worse than the traditional beating.

Emma's stepmother would always say the same things when she was getting tired and the beating was almost over. . . Emma knew the routine.

Maureen would scream, "Have you had enough? Are you going to be good?"

"Yes, yes!" Emma would cry.

Emma was used to the routine of Maureen's beatings. It was always the same. She would yell the same sentence at her, and Emma's response would always be the same. Except for the one time when Maureen changed the script, and unfortunately, Emma gave the wrong response.

Maureen's arm was getting tired. She had been hitting Emma with the yardstick for a while. Katie and Amy were knelt beside Emma and Maureen, watching.

It was horrible to be beaten, but even worse to be beaten while lying on the floor as Katie and Amy watched.

Maureen squatted on her knees above Emma. Emma lay on her stomach on the cool linoleum floor, her arms splayed out in front of her.

As if a dark demon had taken hold of her, Maureen screamed at Emma, "Are you going to be good?"

Over and over, Maureen beat the wooden yardstick, with all her strength, against Emma's back, bottom and legs. It was as if Maureen was beating some unseen force, someone or something other than the eight-year-old little girl lying on the floor in front of her.

The beating was almost over, Emma knew, because the blows were not as hard now. She knew that at any moment Maureen would say, *Are you going to be good? Have you had enough?* And Emma would respond,

Yes, just as she always did. That was what Maureen wanted to hear, that Emma would be good and that she'd had enough.

Emma thought that Maureen felt in control and powerful when she beat her. Since she was married to Dean, a wife and child beating man, it was probably one of the few times she did feel in control of her life.

Emma felt the cold hard floor under her hipbones, knees and elbows. She was exhausted from the pain, humiliation, and sadness of what her stepmother was doing to her. She wanted to go off by herself, away from her family, when she heard Maureen say, "Do you want some more?"

Instantly Emma blurted out, "Yes," not realizing that Maureen had just changed the script. Emma thought she was going to say, *Have you had enough? Are you going to be good?* just as she always did. Immediately, but too late, Emma realized her mistake as Maureen began beating her with renewed energy.

That afternoon, the beating went on much longer than usual, all because Emma had heard wrong and had given Maureen the wrong response.

It was not easy being a child with a hearing disorder. Emma could have avoided that extra beating if only she would have heard her stepmother more clearly. Emma had found that she could better understand what people were saying if she watched their mouths. Unfortunately, while she was getting any one of the variety of beatings from her parents, she was standing away from Maureen or Dean's faces and she couldn't hear what they were saying. She relied on the routine of what they usually said.

Sometimes, Emma was just as scared of Maureen as she was of Dean. There were times she would become so angry at her life with Dean and his children that Maureen would grab Emma by the shoulders and shake her until she felt like her head would shake right off her shoulders. Maureen shook her so much, and so hard, that sometimes when Maureen wasn't shaking Emma, it felt as if her body was still convulsing, and she would feel like her body was shaking all on its own. The shaking sensation would come over her unexpectedly. The room would feel as if it were shaking back and forth, real fast. She would hold her hands out as if warding off some invisible force, shaking back and forth faster and faster as a roaring sound rushed in her ears. The shaking feeling would last for about a minute and she would be forced to stop whatever she was doing until the sensation was gone. After the shaking sensation passed, her skin would get a tingly feeling starting at her head and face creeping down her body to her toes.

To *avoid* the increasing barrage of physical torment, Emma looked for places around the house to hide. A refrigerator box in one of the spare rooms upstairs was her favorite hiding place and she had another hiding place downstairs, in the green room, one of the many rooms in the house that was never used.

There was a green couch, a green chair, and a wooden bookshelf which held the children's school photo albums, and a Buddha statue. It was a pretty room, the nicest room in the entire house, so Emma didn't understand why Maureen and Dean never went in there, and why they didn't put their family's TV in the room. Because no one ever went into the room, it became one of Emma's hideout safe-places. She could sit quietly in the green room, behind the green chair, for hours just to get away from Maureen and Dean.

But one day, Maureen found Emma hiding in the green room, curled up behind the green chair. Emma didn't hear Maureen walk across the plush carpet in the room. All of sudden, Maureen was there beside her, grabbing Emma's arm as she pulled her to her feet. Maureen began shaking Emma, and didn't stop until the little girl saw spots before her eyes, and felt dizzy. She felt the blood pounding in her head.

Emma knew when Maureen lost it, she wasn't really mad at *her*. Maureen was miserable because Dean didn't only beat Emma but he beat Maureen, too. Dean was filled with dark rage and beating Emma was like a release valve for him, but he beat his wife as well, beat her in front of their children.

Emma was sitting in front of the tree, cross-legged, in the front yard, facing the road away from the house. She knew that no one in the house on Third Street could see her. It was one of her outside hiding places; at least she did not think anyone in the house could see her. Katie and Amy walked into her line of vision as if they knew she would be sitting there, leaned against the tree. Emma looked up at her sisters.

"We need to talk to you about something," Katie said as she looked down at her little sister.

Emma did not say anything, just continued to stare up at her sisters.

"In our room," Katie said.

Emma uncrossed her legs and climbed to her feet, and followed her sisters across the lawn, up the stairs to the porch, up the stairs to their bedroom, and sat on her bed. She was curious as to what the mystery was all about, but suspected she already knew.

"You have to be careful," Katie said. "'Don't go anywhere alone with our dad because he does bad things."

"Yeah," Amy said, "real bad things."

7

Eight-year-old Emma sat on the couch by the too-big-for-their-living-room brown wooden table, and waited. Her chores had been completed hours ago just as Maureen had asked. Earlier that morning, Maureen told Katie, Amy and Emma that they had to do an extra good job with their chores of dusting all of the furniture, sweeping all of the floors and cleaning the bathroom. She had explained that the house had to be extra clean because a doctor was going to pay a visit to their house that afternoon to talk to Amy. The doctor, she explained, was going to help Amy stop wetting the bed. Bedwetting wasn't something Amy had always done, it was a recent thing, and Maureen was just *sick* of it. Amy was nine years old, too big to be wetting the bed, Maureen said. She was hoping the doctor could tell her why Amy was wetting the bed, and help end the problem.

Emma thought she knew why Amy was wetting the bed. Dean. It was *his* fault she was wetting the bed and had to wear a diaper at night. He was literally scaring and hurting the pee right out of her. What Emma didn't understand was why Maureen was so mad and mean to Amy about it. Maybe Maureen was going to have the doctor talk to Dean, to make him stop hurting Amy, Katie, and even her because he certainly did not listen to *Maureen*.

Maureen had been a bundle of nervous energy all morning, and was now pacing around the small living room, occasionally walking to the door to look out the window. She had just sat down on her rocking chair when there was a knock at the door. She practically leapt off the seat of the chair, Emma noticed, and rushed to open the door to let a strange man into the room. They spoke in hushed tones for a few minutes and then she called for Amy to join them as they walked down the hall. Emma wondered if they were going to their bedroom to talk about all the bad stuff, or if they were going to the green room. They had not instructed Emma to follow them so she remained on the couch, her hands folded on her lap, wondering if she would need to talk to the doctor next.

As Emma waited for whatever would happen next, she thought about Amy and Dean, and the footsteps at night. Emma tagged along behind Amy sometimes, even when it bugged her sister, but she thought it might help to have her nearby. She saw the things that happened in the house, to her sisters, and tried to be invisible so Dean would leave her alone, wouldn't touch her that way. She hoped the doctor would save Amy, save them all from Dean.

Emma was surprised that the doctor did not stay for very long and didn't talk to anyone else but Amy. Maybe Maureen was in a hurry to get the doctor out of the house before Dean returned home, Emma considered. Emma suspected that Dean would be angry, *very* angry, if he knew there was a doctor in the house talking to Amy.

The doctor did not glance at the other Snow children sitting quietly on the couch when he walked back into the room. He left quietly, and quickly. The doctor never came back to visit Amy or any of the other children that lived in the house on Third Street, and neither did any other doctor.

8

Ten-year-old Emma was lying on her stomach on the warm sidewalk under the large old oak tree in front of the house on Third Street. She was sleepy from her fearful night the night before. The ghostly footsteps had kept her awake. Emma yawned.

Lazily, she watched as a fuzzy black caterpillar wiggled its way across the cracked sidewalk.

"Let's play hopscotch!" Amy insisted, and tossed a rock in front of Emma, just missing the caterpillar.

Emma looked up at her older sister and noticed the dark smudges beneath her eyes, and the scowl wrinkling her face. She suspected that her older sister hadn't slept much the night before either; the sounds of the house must have kept her awake, too.

"Okay," Emma sighed, and rolled from her stomach to her back then climbed to her feet.

Together, the girls used rocks to draw faint lines, creating their hopscotch game. Then they half-heartedly began their game of jumping from square to square with the correct placement of their rocks in squares.

As the shadows grew longer, the game of hopscotch forgotten, Amy and Emma knew they would soon hear their stepmother calling them in for supper. They heard a high-pitched voice. It was the neighbor calling her kids in for supper. Amy and Emma looked up and looked across the street, and watched their friends run into their house.

Emma looked down at the flower necklace she had been working on, and tied the final flower in place. She smiled at her handiwork, at her lovely necklace. The flowers were pink and white, but she knew that by morning, the petals would have turned brown, and she'd have to make a new one.

"Amy, Emma. Supper time!" Maureen shouted.

Looking up from her flower necklace, Emma saw her stepmother standing on the front porch, a towel hanging loosely from one hand. Maureen was dressed as she always was, in shorts, what looked like a man's worn-out t-shirt and a pair of brown loafers. Such an ugly, outfit, Emma thought as she climbed slowly to her feet, especially the brown shoes. Maureen was the only woman Emma knew that wore brown loafers with shorts.

Emma stared with dread up at the house as she walked toward the wooden porch. Amy bolted past her and ran up the steps and into the house, the black screen door slamming behind her. Knowing it would be very bad for her to be late for supper, Emma ran across the yard towards the house. If she was the last one seated at the table it would be reason enough for Dean to knock her off of her chair.

In one motion, Emma tossed the necklace onto the porch and pulled open the screen door. The door slammed behind Emma as she ran down the hall. She walked into the warm living room and then into the even warmer kitchen where Maureen was busy putting the meal on the table. Emma looked at the food being placed on the table, at the roast—she hated slimy roast—corn, green beans, and biscuits for dinner, and milk. Warm milk, Emma thought. She hated warm milk. Maureen saved time by pouring the tall glasses of milk and placing them on the table while she finished cooking. By the time everyone sat down to eat supper, the milk had grown warm.

Katie and Amy, her little sister Laura, and her younger brothers Robby and Timmy, and Dean were already sitting at the table. Everyone was in their assigned seat, with the baby, Timmy, sitting in the highchair. Dean was sitting at the head of the table, to the right of Emma, close enough for him to reach out and hit her. Why, Emma wondered, did she always have to sit next to him? She wanted to sit as far away as possible, out of his reach.

She had already done something she tried so hard not to do and she wasn't even sitting down yet. She was late to supper.

Dean turned toward Emma as he raised a fork full of beans towards his mouth.

With his mouth full of food, he asked, "Where you been? Didn't you hear Maureen callin' you?"

Emma wanted to melt into the room, become one with the chair she was sitting on. She hunched her shoulders and avoided making eye contact with Dean. For a reason that Emma could not explain, she was Dean's target of fury. He punched her face, pounded her head into the walls of the house, and would threaten her with a whippin', and often followed through with one of his very violent whippin's. After he unleashed his fury on her body, it was as if his demons had been freed, and for a few days, he was at peace, and she was safe from him.

Nervously, Emma began to eat her supper. As she listened to her family talk about their day, she speared a green bean with her fork, and then sucked it into her mouth. She stabbed a piece of the slimy roast and popped it into her mouth. As she chewed, she reached her hand toward her cup—placed to the right of her plate—needing to quickly wash down the meat. Grasping the cup with one hand, Emma brought it to her lips and took a drink, swallowing some of the warm milk. As she set the heavy, almost full, glass of milk back onto the table in front of her, it began to tip. She tried to get a tighter grip on the cup and watched in horror as it toppled onto its side. Warm creamy milk spilled all over her end of the table, right in front of Dean's plate. A miniature milk waterfall trickled over the side of the table and pooled onto the floor below.

Emma froze. She didn't breath. Stupid—*stupid*, she thought.

Dean stood up so fast he knocked his chair over. He pulled his arm back to get good momentum and then smacked Emma's face with his open hand. She didn't really feel pain from the force of the blow; it was more of a shocked stunned sensation. It was almost as if the nerve endings in her face had died from the blows to her face she had received over the years.

The force of the blow caused her to lose her balance, and she fell down between the chairs, half on, and half off. She couldn't hear what Dean was shouting at her because of the humming sound in her right ear, the side of her face where he had hit her. She pulled herself back up onto the chair and hunched her shoulders, preparing for another blow. Emma didn't look up at her family but she knew they were all watching her as Dean continued to yell at her.

"Why are you so damn stupid?" Dean shouted.

"I don't know," Emma mumbled. She looked down at her hands folded on her lap.

Emma wished she could disappear at that moment, somewhere where people weren't always hitting her.

As Maureen cleaned up the milk, she shot angry looks at Emma, angry that she had upset Dean. It was quiet during the rest of supper. No one said a word as everyone shoveled food into their mouths, wanting to be excused as quickly as possible. After Emma had eaten everything on her plate, even forcing the slimy, gagging fat from the roast down her throat, she sat very quietly. She didn't look up or leave the table until Dean had left the room. After he had left the room, she hoped he was not on his way outside to get a stick from the tree. She knew what a stick meant, a beating, with bruises lasting for about a week after to serve as a reminder. When Dean did not come back, Emma knew it was safe to leave the room.

Dean was in a bad temper for the rest of the evening and Emma was sent to her bedroom early while everyone else stayed up and watched TV together. It wasn't so bad, she thought. At least it was still light outside when she walked up the long staircase to her bedroom to get dressed for bed. She knew she would be asleep before the darkness arrived.

Emma was spending more time alone in the bedroom she shared with her sisters, either sent to bed early because Dean was mad at her or because of one of her horrible headaches. She would lie on her bed as her head pounded in time with her heartbeat. She would apply pressure with her hands as tight as she could, and with tears burning her eyes, she would wish the pain of her life and in her head, away.

9

For ten-year-old Emma, the physical pain of being beaten by Dean paled in comparison to the emotional pain she endured. Dean's beatings were either spontaneous or calculated, both types of beatings delivered under the guise of punishments for some unknown infraction Emma had committed. Spontaneous beatings were over quickly, and consisted of Dean punching Emma about the head and face, as if she were a man in a bar room brawl, or he would grab her by her long hair and beat her head into a wall of the house. Calculated beatings were an event, lasting sometimes a half an hour, and took hours to execute, and various items were used to beat her with, such as a belt, or stick. During calculated beatings, Dean would insist that the entire family be present to watch.

One summer afternoon, Emma and her little sister, Laura, were playing under the shade tree in the front yard. They were using sticks to dig holes for the dolls they were playing with. It was an unusually peaceful afternoon at the house on Third Street. All the children were occupied with play as Maureen hung clothes on the clothesline, and Dean puttered in the yard at the opposite side of the house. It was one of the good days.

Emma looked up at the sky from where she was crouched near Laura, and watched a fluffy cloud drift lazily in the brilliant blue sky. She felt the warm summer breeze on her bare arms and legs, and looked at the leaves sway on the branches overhead and then felt the searing sting in her eyes from the dirt that Laura had thrown at her. Pressing the balls of her hands to her eyes, she stumbled to her feet.

"What'd you do that for, you brat?" Emma shouted at her five-year-old little sister.

Tears ran down her cheeks from the pain. Emma looked down at her little sister who was grinning and staring up at her.

Laura stuck out her tongue at Emma.

Her favorite sister, Emma thought in surprise. Her cute little sister had just thrown dirt at her. Laura had waist-length chestnut colored hair, and was typically a sweet natured five-year-old, and cherished by each of her three older sisters. Laura could always find a seat on a lap when watching TV, and someone to read a story to her, or a companion to color with her.

Emma rubbed her eyes and felt dirt hit her legs. Through burning, watery eyes, she watched Laura grab another handful of dirt and throw it up at her again.

Mean girl, Emma fumed. The house was making her sweet little sister into a meanie, like Maureen and Dean.

"Stop it!" Emma shouted.

"Make me!" Laura shouted up at Emma.

Her eyes still burning, Emma knelt down, grabbed a handful of dirt, and threw it on her little sister, knowing the second the dirt left her hand she had just made a very big mistake, one that she would dearly regret.

Laura screamed an ear-piercing scream as she leapt to her feet and bolted toward the side of the house.

Panicking, Emma ran after her.

"Laura! Wait! I'm sorry!" Emma shouted after Laura.

Emma rounded the corner of the house and saw Laura crying to Maureen that Emma had thrown dirt on her. Tears were streaming down Laura's cheeks.

Maureen knelt down in front of Laura and wiped her long hair away from her face, and then wiped her tears. Maureen turned toward Emma and glared at her.

"She threw dirt at me first," Emma said, knowing she was in real trouble. Her heart was pounding as she wondered who would beat her this time, Dean or Maureen.

"She's just a little girl!" Maureen shouted.

"I know," Emma said. And Emma did know it was stupid to get mad at her little sister. "I'm sorry!"

"Get in the house!" Maureen insisted as she picked Laura up and walked toward the other side of the house where Emma knew Dean was working.

It would be Dean, Emma realized, who beat her. In fear, she walked to the side door and walked up the steps to wait for her punishment.

Emma walked into the empty living room and sat down on the orange footstool, and waited. Within minutes, Dean walked into the room, with Maureen following behind carrying Laura. Katie, Amy and Robby followed behind.

"Do you wanna whippin'?!" Dean bellowed.

Slowly Emma looked up, up at Dean's black combat boots, his blue jeans, black belt, brown t-shirt, and lastly at his face, his purposeful, furious face.

She was terrified, felt hysteria rise up inside her; her thoughts a jumble and her tongue-tied like a shoelace. Did she want a whippin', she considered, fear taking her breath away. Not particularly. Her throat felt like an earthworm stuck to the sidewalk on a hot summer afternoon. She tried to work up some spit to moisten her throat.

"No," she whispered.

Dean must not have heard her because he repeated the question.

"Do you wanna whippin'?"

Emma shook her head, no.

"No," she said, her voice quivering. Tears burned her eyes, and this time not from dirt, but from sheer terror.

Emma watched Dean walk to the kitchen. He picked up the chair from the head of the kitchen table and carried it back to the living room, placing it in the center of the room.

Katie, Amy, Laura, Maureen and Robby stood near the couch, in a line. All eyes were on Dean as he slowly pulled his black belt through the loops of his jeans.

The skin on Emma's face tingled and she felt as if she might wet her pants.

The sharp crack of the belt broke the silence in the room.

Emma jumped.

"Do you wanna whippin'?" Dean asked, lowering his deep voice to a growl.

"No," Emma whispered as she stared at the leather belt.

"Get up," Dean commanded.

Emma rose to her feet, but didn't walk toward him.

Dean cracked the belt again.

"The belt or a switch?" Dean asked.

Emma licked her dry lips. She flinched when she heard the belt crack again.

The belt he held in his hand or a stick off of the tree in the front yard? Emma panicked. The tree was where Dean hung the deer he killed during hunting season, its guts gone, and blood dripping from its body. The belt or a stick, both would create bruises where they landed on her tender skin. Neither better than the other. Both burned as they dug into her flesh.

Dean decided for her. He sat down on the chair.

"Git over here," Dean growled.

Emma forced her legs to carry her to Dean, and stood in front of him, their eyes meeting. She could see the rest of her family out of the corner of her eye, all of them standing to the left of her.

"Pull your pants down," Dean instructed as he looked straight into Emma's face.

Emma's face burned with embarrassment.

"Pull 'em down," Dean said when she didn't move.

Emma tucked her thumbs into the waistband of her shorts and pushed down, stopping when her thumbs touched just below the cheeks of her bottom.

"Farther," he said as he stared into her eyes.

Tears burned Emma's eyes as she pushed her shorts down the back of her legs. Emma noticed how silent it was in the room, as if she and Dean were alone but she knew her sisters, brother and Maureen were there, watching her humiliation. She wished they would look away, but knew if they did, they would have a turn standing in front of the crazy, mean man.

Emma straightened, spreading her legs apart a little, so that her shorts would not fall to the floor, needing to be covered as much as possible.

"All the way down," Dean said. "And your underwear."

Emma didn't move.

Dean cracked the belt.

It felt to Emma as if the air had been sucked out of the room. Her face felt as if it was on fire. Tucking her thumbs into the band of her underwear, she pulled down, stopping at just beneath the cheeks of her bottom, keeping her little girl parts covered.

"*All* the way," Dean said, his voice deeper.

Emma allowed her shorts and underwear to fall to the tops of her feet, now standing half-naked in front of everyone in the room.

"Bend over," Dean instructed, indicating she was to bend over his knees.

Emma shuffled to the side of his body, careful not to lose her shorts and underwear off the tops of her feet. Once she was standing in the correct beating position, Emma stood on her tiptoes and then leaned over Dean's knees, her bare bottom exposed and facing her stepmother, sisters and brother.

She tensed her legs and bottom, stealing her body for the first blow, but nothing could prepare her mind or body for the burning pain of the belt.

Emma knew each time a blow was coming. She felt the shift of Dean's body when he reached his arm back, and then the forward motion as his arm propelled his hand and belt forward onto her bottom and legs, and even her back when his aim was not accurate. She did not cry out in pain, knowing that screams fueled him, caused the beating to last longer, the belt landing more times on her body. She lost count of the times the belt hit their tender mark, over ten times, and when he was finished with his summer afternoon sport, he pushed his daughter off of his lap.

Emma scrambled to pull her underwear and shorts over her bruised body, and equally bruised spirit, the welts on her skin already visible.

Emma stood in front of Dean, her hands clasped in front of her, waiting until he left the room, knowing then, she too, could be excused. She, along with everyone else in the room, watched as he snaked the black belt back through the loops of his jeans. Then he walked toward the kitchen, intent on pouring a glass of iced tea.

Once he had left the room, Emma, red faced, walked toward the hall, wanting to go to her bedroom and be alone with her humiliation and pain.

The air was heavy with the heat of the afternoon when Emma walked into her bedroom. She clicked on the wooden, homemade box fan at the foot of her bed, and then curled up onto her side on her bed, tucking a hand under her flat pillow that cradled her head.

Several minutes later, Emma felt a hand on her shoulder.

"I'm sorry," Laura said, softly.

Emma remained upstairs for the remainder of the day, for a while snuggled next to the pillow on her bed, and then in the giant room at the end of the hall. Maureen had constructed a playroom out of a refrigerator box, and it was there Emma lay, dizzy from the heat. She didn't want to be around any of her family, not her sisters, little brothers, Dean or Maureen. If she was alone, she reasoned, she couldn't get into trouble, and with that thought, Emma fell into a deep sleep for several hours.

Later that night, lying next to Laura on the bed they shared, Emma had difficulty falling asleep. Even though the windows in the bedroom were open, and fans blew on Emma and her three sisters, it felt as if she were sleeping in an oven. She could barely breathe, and tossed and turned trying to find a cool spot on the bed. The house seemed to be alive with sound, bumping and banging, and footsteps seemed to echo throughout the room as Emma fell into a fitful sleep.

10

Occasionally, Maureen and Dean went out to dinner with their friends, the Harpers, and left Emma and her little brothers and sisters home with a babysitter. The Harpers were Maureen and Dean's *only* friends and sometimes, they played cards on a Saturday night or went to dinner together in town. The Harper's son was in Katie's class at school, and their daughter was one year younger than Emma was. They were nice kids, friendly and kind, just like their parents.

Maureen and Dean had taken their six children with them to the Harper's home on a few card-playing nights. During the summer, the Harper kids and Snow kids would play outside while the adults played cards at the kitchen table. It was one of the few uncomplicated times of Emma's childhood; cool summer evenings spent catching lightning bugs and playing tag in the dark.

Emma noticed how the Harpers treated one another, watched them when she went into their kitchen for a drink of water during card-playing nights. She saw how it could be—should be—the hand holding and smiles. It was the free-pass-from-beating-Emma evenings. Dean pretended to be someone else while the Snow family was in the Harper home, someone who was not violent and didn't beat his daughter.

Emma loved it when her parents went out for the evening, which was not often enough, in her opinion. Throughout the entire day on date night, Maureen would glide through the day, anticipating an evening of fun with Dean and their friends; so happy, smiling and singing to herself. Those were the good days, parents preoccupied with thoughts of fun, a reprieve from the darkness that had enveloped their lives.

Emma was excited that Maureen and Dean were going to go out tonight with the Harpers. Dean and Maureen had already taken turns showering in the small bathroom off the kitchen, the bathroom with the hole in the plastic door. It was a steamy evening, Emma's neck sticky from the heat. The air was so heavy, it felt as if it was lodged in her chest making it difficult to breathe. While Dean was drinking a glass of iced tea, Emma heard him tell Maureen that a thunderstorm would break the oppressive heat weather pattern that had blanketed the town for the last two weeks. Emma didn't like thunderstorms, knowing that they could quickly become deadly tornadoes, and didn't like the booming thunder and bright light of lightening.

Maureen walked through the living room wearing only her slip, and underwear beneath, trying to find relief from the afternoon heat. She walked to the closet in her bedroom and slid blouses and the few dresses she owned, along the rod. Nothing to wear, she decided. She walked to the green room where she kept her special things stored away, intent on digging through boxes to find an old dress to wear tonight. The pitter-patter of four little girls followed behind her. Perhaps the old peach dress and high-heeled peach shoes to match, she mused.

After carefully sifting through a cardboard box, Maureen stood up and faced the Snow girls.

"What do you think?" Maureen asked, and held up a peach dress in one hand and shoes to match in the other.

The little girls sat on the floor in the green room looking up at Maureen, dreamy-eyed as they thought how beautiful their mother would be in the peach dress, so very different from her usual work outfits. Maureen had started working at Caterpillar—a factory—on Emma's birthday that year. It was nothing like the secretary job she had when she was 18, when she first met Dean. Then, she had worn beautiful dresses and shoes to work, and carried purses to match, but now it was a hot greasy kind of job and she dressed to be safe and comfortable instead of pretty. Emma and her sisters liked it when Maureen got dressed up in pretty things, transforming into a modern-day Cinderella, except Dean was no Prince Charming. The peach dress it would be, Maureen decided. She hoped she dazzled Dean with how pretty she looked and that nothing would set off one of his dark moods.

Maureen leaned toward the bathroom mirror over the sink as she applied her makeup. She felt the coolness of the sink through her slip which, besides the inside of the small, old relic of a refrigerator, was the only cool thing in the house. Even the fans were not doing the job this afternoon. They were just blowing the hot around.

Emma watched as Maureen smeared makeup all over her face. The small room smelled of Covergirl makeup. The young girl was fascinated as she watched her stepmother use what looked like a paintbrush to apply green eye shadow to one eyelid, and then the other. Emma squinted her eyes as she watched Maureen apply black eye liner, and then watched as she pulled a mascara wand through her lashes, making them magically longer and thicker. Emma watched as Maureen picked up a tube of lipstick. The tube of lipstick made a popping sound when she opened it. Maureen wound the tube until the pink tip peeked out of the gold colored metal tube. Then she rubbed it over her upper and then her lower lip. She smacked her lips in completion. Then, one by one, Maureen placed all of her magical beauty products back into the bag that she kept them in and then slid the bag back into the cubbyhole by the sink, where it belonged.

Maureen shooed Emma out of the bathroom, and followed behind her, a smile on her lips, and humming a little tune. A few minutes later, Maureen glided into the living room where the children were watching television. She twirled in a circle.

"What do you think?" Maureen asked, smiling. "How do I look?"

The scent of Maureen's perfume drifted across the room to Emma, tickling her nose. It was a nice smell, the smell of a happy Maureen.

Emma and her sisters told Maureen that she looked beautiful in her peach colored knee-length sleeveless dress with matching pumps, because she was beautiful. Maureen's face glowed with happiness.

When Dean walked out of the bedroom, Maureen turned toward her husband, grinned and placed her hands on her hips. Emma could smell Dean's aftershave from across the room. His aftershave was not nice, nothing like the scent of Maureen's perfume. His was an uncomfortable scent. Old Spice, Emma thought, and wrinkled her nose in disgust.

Tina, Emma's cousin, had already arrived to babysit. She was several years older than Katie was, and had babysat during date nights before. Emma liked it when Tina came over. She was fun, and shared stories about her boyfriends and the parties she went to. They watched movies, ate bowls of popcorn, and drank pop, and she allowed the children to stay up past their bedtime

Emma glanced at the clock. Typically, on date night, Maureen and Dean were out long after she was asleep. She was seated on the floor with a bowl of popcorn on her lap, watching the late movie with Tina, Katie, Amy and Laura. She had stayed up much later when Tina babysat and it wasn't really late yet, but she was beginning to feel uneasy. She didn't want to be up when Dean got home, knew that if he saw his children lounging around his living room after a nice night out, it could end their night very badly. It had been such a nice day; Emma didn't want it spoiled by getting a whippin' and she was sure as late as it was, that he would use his belt or his fist, no sticks tonight. Emma looked toward the side door, then glanced at the clock again. Her heart began to beat a little bit faster. Then she saw it. Lights. Lights flashed across the dark living room, which moments before had been lit only be the TV they had been watching.

Tina saw the car headlights from Dean's car as it pulled up to the side of the house at the same time Emma did. She knew Dean had an explosive temper. Jumping to her feet, Tina snatched a bowl of popcorn off the floor and as many cups as she could carry.

"Move! Move! Get up stairs! Hurry! Hurry—before they get inside the house. Go! Go!" Tina whispered as loud as she dared.

Emma was already on her feet and running toward the heavy wood door that would be her escape to the stairs to her bedroom. Katie pulled the door closed as Dean and Maureen walked into the living room.

Tina's voice was muffled through the heavy door.

"Hi. Did you have a good time?" Tina asked.

Emma detected the nervousness in Tina's voice. She heard Dean shout something, but she couldn't make out what it was he was yelling about. Perhaps he had figured out that his children were not yet in bed.

He continued to yell, and then she heard a familiar sound, the sound of fists on face. Then, Maureen's voice as she screamed. Likely, Emma thought, he was hitting Maureen. Their night must not have gone well.

The Snow girls looked at one another, wide-eyed and scared. They remained at the door for a few minutes more, heard something, or someone thrown into a wall, and another scream.

"Dean, stop!" Tina screamed. "Stop it! Stop it!"

Emma heard something hit the floor and the sound of a bell. Dean must have thrown the telephone. Maybe Tina was trying to call her dad, Emma considered, to come help Maureen.

Maureen was still screaming as Emma and her sisters ran as quietly as possible up the stairs to their bedroom, hoping the creaking of the stairs would not be heard over the racket down below.

Quietly, Katie shut the bedroom door, but it didn't shut out the sounds from the room below. Maureen's sobs drifted up to Emma's bedroom. The sounds of things being thrown, Dean's shouting and Maureen sobbing scared Emma. It sounded like she was dying.

The girls heard Tina begin to cry and then they heard what sounded like footsteps and the side-door to the house slam. Maureen was still screaming, an ear piercing scream, over and over, but no one came to help her. It must have been Tina that ran out of the house, Emma thought. Eventually Maureen's screams became softer, more of a moaning sound.

The shouting, screaming, and crying went on for what seemed like hours. Emma lay in the dark of her bedroom, curled up on her side, her heart thudding in her chest hoping he wouldn't come upstairs to get her next. She prayed to Jesus to make Dean stop hurting Maureen.

"Please, Jesus, protect us," Emma whispered.

Sometime in the middle of the night, the shouting stopped. It was quiet. Exhausted, the girls fell asleep.

The next morning, Emma and her sisters remained in their bedroom as long as they could. They were afraid to go downstairs to see what Dean had done to Maureen. The only bathroom in the house was on the first floor, so eventually they had no choice but to go downstairs.

As Emma stood in the doorway to the kitchen, she was surprised to see that the metal cabinet doors that had always hung in place, until now, were gone. Dean must have ripped them away in a fit of rage the evening before, ripped them right off the hinges. All the dishes—plates and glasses—and boxes of food were exposed. Well, Emma thought, that explains what one of the banging sounds were the night before. She wondered who he was going to blame for the missing cabinet doors. Dean would have to replace them and even though he had been stupid enough to rip them off, he would blame someone else for the absence. Someone else would pay the price for the missing doors, and most likely, it would be taken out on Emma.

Emma looked around the room and saw Maureen standing by the stove, facing away from her, cooking Dean's breakfast. She smelled bacon and eggs frying in the black iron skillet.

Dean sat at the kitchen table. He had dried blood on his hands. He looked up at each of his daughters, looked at each of them one by one.

"It's her fault." Dean nodded his head toward Maureen. "It's her fault there's no doors. She made me cut my hands. Look at 'em. I probably need stitches."

He wanted his children to feel sorry for his swollen, torn, and bloody hands.

"It's because of her that I had to rip 'em off," Dean said, meaning the cabinet doors.

Maureen turned toward the table and placed a plate of fried eggs, toast, and bacon in front of Dean. Emma tried to look into Maureen's face but she looked down, not wanting to catch anyone's eye. Emma could see that her lip was bleeding, and her cheek was swollen and purple. The evidence of the beating from the night before was mottled along Maureen's bare arms. Large bruises marked her otherwise creamy colored skin.

A great sadness enveloped Emma for Maureen. Her heart cried. Emma's head snapped toward Dean. She tried to gauge his mood, wondering if at any second he might become violent, or had his fury subsided. One small clumsy move on her part could be the spark that reignited the flame of fury.

After the children shoveled down the cold cereal they were eating for breakfast, they returned to the bedroom and did not come out for the rest of the day, except to eat and use the bathroom. There were no squabbles between the girls that day, and when they did speak to one another, it was in hushed tones. Emma was scared. No one had come to save Maureen last night, not her uncle or the neighbors. No one cared. Dean could do what he wanted and no one would help.

Later that afternoon, rain began to fall, thunder rumbled and a cool breeze blew through the house on Third Street.

11

It was early August, and within a month, Emma would be starting fifth grade. Dean wanted to drive to Arkansas to visit his brother before school started, at least that was what Emma had overheard him say to Maureen. Her first vacation, Emma mused, did not start off well at all. If she never took another vacation with her family, it would be fine with her.

Ten-year-old Emma felt, and smelled, her three sister's and little brother's sweat, and felt a bony elbow and knee dig into her when the truck hit a bump on the road. The Snow children had been crammed into the back of Dean's pickup truck before the sun had come up that morning, and before the heat of the day had rolled in like a storm. Now, it was hot and dusty in the back of the truck.

The night before, Dean, with Maureen's help, had drug an old stained mattress into the back of the truck. It didn't quite lay flat on the bed of the truck, instead it folded up around the sides. The family didn't have a car large enough to haul all six children, two adults and luggage needed for the one week they planned to stay in Arkansas with Dean's older brother and his family on his ranch. At four that morning, the five oldest children were lined up at the back end of the truck. And one by one they had climbed into the back of the navy blue truck, careful not to bump their heads on the low hanging topper.

During the first few hours of the trip, it was still dark outside and the movement of the truck lulled the children to sleep. But when the sun began climbing in the sky, beating down on the topper of the truck, the children began to feel as if they were slowly roasting, just like a chicken for Sunday dinner, which resulted in hot, and very irritable children. The children couldn't get comfortable; they were hot, hungry, and while the topper of the truck was tall enough for a child to sit up straight, they toppled into one another if the truck swerved or hit a bump on the highway.

Emma heard Dean swear, and felt the truck swerve hard to the right, toppling the bodies in the back of the truck onto one another. Those that had been sitting upright were now toppled onto their sides. He pulled the truck over to the side of the highway. The Snow children knew that was not a good thing; they knew that one of them was going to get it.

When Dean opened the topper, light burst into the back of the truck. The children squinted in the blinding light.

"What the fuck is goin' on back here?" Dean demanded to know. "Who is it?"

Impatiently, Dean did not wait for any of the children to answer.

"Emma. It's Emma isn't it," he insisted. "Keep your fucking hands to yourself!"

Emma hunched down like a beaten dog. She wasn't touching anyone, she thought, at least no more on purpose than anyone else was. It was difficult not to actually touch each other when five kids were laying on a small mattress.

"Did yuh hear me?" Dean shouted.

Emma shook her head yes, and looked up at him, her body still slouched in a submissive position. He was yelling only at her, she thought. She was embarrassed but angry, too, because she hadn't done anything wrong. At that moment, Emma wasn't afraid of Dean. She didn't think he'd yank her out of the back end of the truck and beat her alongside the highway. Someone might see. Dean didn't beat Emma in front of his neighbors or his friends, or anyone in town, because he wanted them to think he was a nice man. And she didn't think he would beat her alongside the road, but it was still humiliating to be yelled at in front of her family.

Always, me, Emma thought, wishing Dean would just get back in the truck and keep driving.

"Come here," Dean said.

Emma looked up in surprise.

"Come *here*," Dean said.

On her hands and knees, Emma crept forward, climbing over bodies as she moved toward Dean. As she crawled, the old familiar terror washed over her. Maybe he *was* going to beat her alongside the highway, she considered.

When she arrived at the foot of the truck bed, she stopped, still on all fours, not sure what he wanted her to do next. Should she try to climb over the back end of the truck and jump down to the road, or should she continue to just sit there? She wasn't sure and didn't want to make him any madder than he already was by doing the wrong thing.

"Come *here!*" Dean shouted.

She was *here,* she thought. She inched forward.

Dean took a swing at Emma's face with his fist. Emma flinched, shifting her weight. His fist barely made contact with her jaw.

"Sit still," Dean commanded.

Emma was kneeling now, her toes bracing her so she wouldn't be knocked over when Dean punched her. Sit still, she thought. So he *wasn't* going to beat her alongside the highway. He had plenty of room to do a quick beating, as he stood right outside of the truck. How convenient, she thought, dully.

She braced her face. Clenched her teeth, willing herself to be perfectly still as Dean's fist plowed into the side of her face, hard enough to rattle her teeth. Bright, white light danced before her eyes, and she felt a burning pain on the side of her face, down her jawbone. Emma continued sitting in punch receiving positon as Dean lowered the topper door back into place, and then latched it. Only after Dean had walked around the truck, slid onto his seat and pulled the truck onto the highway, did

Emma move. Without a word, or glance at her brother and sisters, Emma scooted to the nearest edge of the mattress and lay down, curling onto her side. The Snow children were subdued after that. There were no more complaints of being touched, being too hot, and no complaints of being hungry. The truck was quiet for the rest of the drive to Arkansas, to their first and only vacation destination as a family.

Emma was thankful when summer was over and the new school year began. It meant time away from home, but not enough time. She still had to endure evenings and weekends at the house on Third Street.

Fourth grade had been a wonderful school year for Emma, an escape from life at home. Her teacher had been kind, the classwork had been easy for her, and the kids in her class had been nice. The teacher had shared her love of the Laura Ingalls Wilder books, had read the first of the Little House on the Prairie books to the class. Emma could have sat all day long listening to her teacher read the story. After the teacher finished the book, and she shared that there were more Little House on the Prairie books, Emma checked them out of the school's library and had read all of them by the end of the year.

Fifth grade, Emma was discovering, was not going to be as easy for her as fourth grade had been, and her new teacher was not as kind. Her new teacher was an older, single woman who lived in a little house right across the street from the house on Third Street. Mrs. Broker, was her fifth grade teacher's name, an older crusty kind of woman who wore old fashioned dresses and shoes from the 1920's, dyed her hair black, and had a pair of cat-eye glasses propped on the bridge of her nose. It wasn't that Mrs. Broker was a mean teacher; she just didn't seem to have much of a personality. She was just . . . there. A cat lady—she was a cat lady type of person.

No matter where the teacher assigned Emma to sit in the classroom, Emma had difficulty seeing the chalkboard, and difficulty hearing instructions, understanding what the teacher said. Emma had had vision and hearing difficulty for years, and past teachers had sent notes home to Dean and Maureen stating that she needed to receive an eye and hearing exam. Mrs. Broker, too, sent a note home to Emma's parents sharing that they needed to get her ears and eyes tested.

Not only was Emma hearing and sight impaired, but she also suffered a speech impediment, the lingering effects from when Dean had almost murdered her when she was three years old. For several years, the elementary school had provided weekly speech therapy to Emma, assisting her in exercising and relearning to use various muscles in her mouth and face.

Emma had known for years that she had a hearing and eyesight disability, knew she couldn't hear and see like the other kids in class. She suspected that it was because her teacher, Mrs. Broker, was their neighbor, that her parents finally felt compelled to take her, and her sister Katie, to see an eye and hearing specialist. Emma had hated attending speech therapy during school because the therapist always arrived during math class, and after therapy, it was almost impossible to catch up to the rest of the class, especially since there was no one to help her with her homework.

One winter afternoon, Emma found herself sitting in an uncomfortable chair at the eye and ear doctor's office, waiting her turn to be seen. She didn't have to wait long before her name was called, and nervously, she walked back to the dark room at the end of the hall. She tried her hardest to pass the hearing test, not wanting to be any more different than she already was. She sat in the little booth and strained to hear the beeps. Her hands became clammy, and her heart pounded with the effort she exerted to hear the faint beeps, or hear any beeps at all, sensing that she should be hearing something. She so badly wanted to raise the shiny silver and blue pen the doctor had given her in the air, indicating that she could hear a sound made by the machine with all of the dials. Emma quickly grew to hate the stupid shiny pen as she strained to hear sound that just could not be heard by the human ear, at least not by her left ear.

When Emma walked out of the small, soundproof room, she sat in a chair next to Dean and Maureen. Within a few minutes, the doctor walked over to Dean and gave him test results, the news that his daughter needed a hearing aid.

Emma watched and listened to the exchange between her parents and the doctor and thought, *no*! There was no way she was going to wear a hearing aid—ever! The kids at school already thought she was different. She couldn't let them find out she was deaf, she thought. Wearing glasses would be bad enough with the kids at school calling her four-eyes but if they found out about the hearing aid, they'd call her a retard.

Lucky me, Emma thought sarcastically, as the doctor made a mold of her ear for her new hearing aid. After the mold of her ear had been created, she was sent back to the waiting room where the receptionist shared that her parents should bring her back in a week to pick *it* up, and her new glasses, too. It was just one more way to show her family what a freak she was, Emma reflected dismally.

After Dean paid the bill, they would be on their way, free from the nauseating office, at least until next week when they would need to come back and pick up the wretched thing. Emma sensed and saw the disgust and anger on Dean's face as he stood at the counter, reached into his back pocket for his black, worn wallet and paid the bill that would help his daughters see better, and help Emma hear again. He was paying to correct the hearing that he had taken from her years before in one of his fits of rage.

Dean didn't want to fork out his money for his children, and he didn't usually. Maureen spent her money for household and child-related expenses. But this time he *was* stuck footing the bill and he was none too happy about it. He would not be paying for Emma's hearing aid and glasses, and Katie's glasses, but for Mrs. Broker's nagging. Aside from being parted from some of his hard-earned money, the fact that he had a special-needs child, bothered him—her disability a reflection on him. To Dean, she was retarded and weak.

The following week, Maureen was unable to get time away from work to take Emma and Katie to pick up their glasses and Emma's hearing aid. It was uncomfortably quiet during the half-hour car ride to the doctor's office. Emma felt the anger in the small space, created by Dean because he was in the driver's seat, literally, taking his daughters to the doctor.

When the doctor balanced Emma's glasses on her nose and ears, for the first time in her memory, she saw crisp detail in the world around her. She was excited to test her new eyes on the book she had brought with her that was waiting for her in the car. Emma was sent back to the waiting room to wait her turn to be fitted for her new hearing aid; several other patients were ahead of her. As she sat down on a chair next to Dean in the waiting room, Emma watched an old lady walk down the hall with the doctor. Old people, Emma observed, wore hearing aids. Little girls did not. They could take all the time they wanted, she thought sourly, because she was in no hurry to look stupid with some bulky thing stuck in her ear. Far too soon to suit Emma, it was her turn to have a bulky beige hearing aid crammed in her ear.

A beige colored, plastic-looking hearing aid rested in the palm of the doctor's hand. Emma stared at it, not touching it. The doctor scooted his chair-on-wheels closer to her and reached toward her ear, tucking a long strand of her hair back out of the way. With his other hand, he wrapped the clear tube over her ear and rested the large beige portion of the hearing aid on the back of her ear, then wiggled the clear tube portion into her ear.

It felt to Emma as if a suction cup had been sealed over her ear, locking out sound.

"You can turn it up or down," the doctor said.

Emma turned her head to the side, feeling as if the contraption in her ear was weighing down her head. A shrill squeal erupted from the hearing aid.

"That's no problem," the doctor said.

He leaned forward and fiddled with Emma's hearing aid.

"It was turned up too loud," the doctor said. "Now you're all set."

Emma reached up and smoothed her hair over her ear. She felt her ear beneath her hair. It was protruding through her hair. Her ear had never stuck out like that before, not before the doctor had stuck the hearing aid onto her ear.

"You are free to go, young lady," the doctor said, and smiled at Emma.

Emma jumped off the chair and followed the doctor to the door, pausing to look in a mirror that had been strategically placed by the door.

Her eyes opened wide when she saw her reflection. Her left ear was sticking out through her hair, like a dolphin's fin sticking up out of the ocean. Tears burned her eyes. Emma pushed on her ear. It popped through her hair again. Her heart beat faster when she realized there was no way to hide the hearing aid. Over and over, Emma tried to smooth her hair over her ear. She scowled at her reflection and then walked out of the room.

During the drive back to school, Emma cracked open her book. It was a magical world of clearly defined words, and when she looked out the car window, she noticed the leaves on trees were different, too. So people could see things clearly far away, she thought, in awe.

She turned her head back to her book, and the squealing sound caused by the hearing aid made her cheeks burn with embarrassment.

A block away from the school, Emma began to panic. Reaching up to her ear, she pushed, held her hand over her ear, attempting to flatten it to her head. But it didn't work. When she smoothed her hand over her hair, she felt the hearing aid where her hair should have been.

How was she going to hide it from the kids in class, she wondered, and her teachers, not realizing that her teachers would have been told where she was that morning.

As she followed Dean into the secretary's office, Emma made sure to stand with her hearing aid-ear away from the secretary. She pulled her hair over the hearing aid, and tilted her head a little so her hair fell to the side. After Dean left, she asked the secretary if she could use the restroom before going back to class, and once safe behind the door of the stall, Emma pealed the hearing aid out of her ear. She turned it off. Heaven forbid it should squeal in her purse, and then tucked it away in a pocket of her over-sized red purse.

A month later, a horrifying incident occurred. Emma's secret was almost exposed. One afternoon she left her red purse in the gymnasium at school. Careless, Emma berated herself as she walked to the office.

Emma had just begun carrying a purse, since she was getting to be that age and a girl never knew when she would need to put those special kinds of things in it. The school had provided the talk about puberty that year and she wanted to be prepared for whatever was going to happen to her, now that she was *that* age. Purse carrying had an added and timely benefit of hiding her hearing aid in the inside pocket.

That afternoon, when Emma walked back into her homeroom class, after lunch and recess, something didn't feel right. The absence of the weight of her purse was what wasn't right. It wasn't there. She panicked when she realized she didn't have it hanging over her shoulder, and reported to her teacher immediately that her very valuable purse, her red purse, was missing. Of course, Ms. Broker understood what a delicate time it was for her female students, knew their might be items of a delicate nature inside the purse, so she sent Emma to find the purse. First stop was the gym. If she didn't find it there, she was to go to the office and check with the secretary to see if anyone had turned it in to the lost and found.

It was the purse of secrets! If anyone opened that purse, Emma thought, horrified, and quickened her pace. She had stuck her hearing aid in the pocket of the purse, just as she did every morning.

Emma checked the bleachers for her purse, and not finding it there, checked the stage for her purse. Nothing. It was not in the gym. Her stomach plummeted. What if someone had her purse and was digging around inside of it right now, she worried. Hopelessly, Emma climbed the worn stairs to the office. It wouldn't be in here, Emma thought. Why would anyone bring a dumb old purse to the office?

"Hello, Emma," the secretary said. "How can I help you?"

Her shoulders slumped in defeat knowing her secret would soon be broadcast over the entire school, Emma looked across the wooden desk that seperated her from the secretarial space.

"Has anyone brought in a purse, a red purse?" Emma asked.

"Why, yes. Someone sure did," the secretary said as she smiled down at Emma. "Let me just go get it for you."

Emma's eyes opened wide with shock as she reached for her oversized red purse.

"Thank you," Emma said. She smiled at the secretary.

"Have a good day, Emma," the secretary said.

With a relieved smile on her face, Emma walked out of the office.

Emma could not believe her luck! It was her lucky day! Then, another thought niggled at her. Did that someone look inside her bag? She stopped in the middle of the hall and hurriedly unzipped her bag, and shoved her hand inside. Her fingertips touched the hearing aid. It was still there. She sighed. But did whoever it was that had found the purse look inside, Emma wondered as she walked back to class. Did someone know her secret?

As Emma walked back into her classroom, she looked at each of the children in the room, all sitting in their assigned seats, some looking at her, some chatting and laughing amongst themselves. Did one of them know, and were they looking at her differently?

Later that evening, Emma came to a decision. That afternoon had been too close a call. There was only one thing she could do. She had to get rid of the hearing aid, she decided. A plan, she needed a plan. The burn barrel behind the bushes at the back of the house would be the perfect plan.

After dinner, Emma carried a sack of garbage to the burn barrel, lit a match and watched the garbage in the can catch fire. She waited until the flames had grown high, and then she tossed the hearing aid into the hot center and waited and watched for a few more minutes to make sure it was completely destroyed.

Emma didn't care what Dean did to her when he found out. The dumb thing didn't work anyway. It just clogged her ear and made her look like a retard. He could beat her if he wanted, but for once in her short-life, she was victorious!

Funny thing, he never saw that *thing* in her ear ever again and never asked her about it.

12

There were many times Emma wondered why she was so very different from Dean, and even different from the mother who abandoned her when she was only two years old. Sometimes, usually after a whippin' or after being punched in the face by Dean, or after a yardstick beating, Emma wondered if perhaps she had been stolen from her real family. She had daydreamed that her real family was probably searching for her. She sighed and flipped onto her stomach on her bed. If only. . .

The summer after her fifth grade year, the abuse began to build; began to take an emotional toll on Emma. She felt empty, felt dead inside. She knew her teachers, aunts, uncles, and neighbors knew Dean was beating her. Her teachers and family could see the purple bruises on the back of her legs, and they could see the effects of abuse on her face, the puffy purple bruises under her eyes from lack of sleep.

Emma hid the bruises on her legs and back as best as she could, tried to hide the humiliation that she was a child who was not loved, but instead a child who was loathed by her parents. She could not face the stares from the other kids at school if they were to see the bruises, knowing that she was so different from them.

PE class became a problem. There were many days of many weeks out of each month that she could not change in front of the other girls because bruises were striped across her lower back, buttocks, backs of her legs and even lower. For days after a beating, it hurt to move, to walk, and place any pressure on the bruises.

Emma found a way to hide the bruises from her teachers and other kids at school. She told the PE teacher that she was on her period, even though she hadn't yet started her period. The teacher didn't make the girls participate in PE during their special time of the month, which meant they didn't have to change into the required PE uniform, shorts and t-shirt. Emma used the excuse frequently and knew her teacher realized something was up, but she was never questioned. She was always excused from participating, excused from changing her clothes in front of the other girls. The teacher had seen the bruises and pretended right along with Emma.

Emma's homeroom teacher, Mrs. Broker, knew what was going on in her house. She knew Dean was beating Emma. Mrs. Broker's small house was situated directly across the street from the Snow family house. Emma speculated that no one really cared what happened to her, and maybe adults did not care about other children, either. If they did care, surely they would save children from men like Dean.

Reading became Emma's escape from the nightmare of her childhood. The fifth grade students at Atlanta Elementary were allowed to visit the library, and check out two books each week when school was in session. The library was accessed by climbing several flights of stairs, on the top floor of the school. Emma was one of the few kids who maximized her library privileges, wishing she could check out more than two books at a time. In the evenings and during weekends, Emma began escaping her life at home. Through the books she read, she went on wonderful journeys, places her family could not find her.

After she finished one book, she immediately began another book. It was how she began passing the time of her childhood, even on beautiful sunny days. She'd find a spot under a cool shade tree and flip page after page of another, much better world.

For Emma's birthday that year, Maureen had given her a book, her very first Nancy Drew mystery. On Emma's birthday that year, Maureen had started her first day at the factory, at Caterpillar, but had left Emma's birthday gifts on the kitchen table. It was the first time Emma had received a book for a gift, and as she flipped the pages, she realized it was a very special gift from a woman who recognized that she needed adventures, friends, and an escape from her life.

The summer before 6th grade, Emma had something to look forward to. Church camp. For one week during the summer, she was going to pretend that she did not live with her crazy dad. Most Sundays, Emma attended the church one block from her house. It was in the same church where she had attended Kindergarten years before and it was because of that church that she was going to be allowed to get away for an entire week.

Emma was shocked that Dean had agreed to allow her to go, that he would agree to let Maureen fork out the money for something God related . . . for her.

After all the years had passed since Emma had lived in the foster home with the grandma foster woman, Emma still hoped that what she had shared was true. She hoped that Jesus would find her and save her. But as time passed, Emma began to lose hope. After all, how difficult was it to find a little girl who lived right down the road from a church?

Emma was extra quiet, and stayed out of the way during the weeks leading up to her trip to church camp. She didn't want to ruin her chance to get away by having Dean cancel the trip. When the day of camp finally arrived, Emma was relieved to see Maureen carry a small suitcase to her bedroom. She packed the one nice dress that she owned, for the church service, and her nicest shorts, tops and one pair of sandals. Maureen had even bought Emma a swimsuit. Emma didn't know how to swim, but she wanted to be like the other girls, so she was sure she would need a suit.

Of course, and thankfully, it was Maureen who drove Emma the long drive through the country to camp. It was a place that Emma had never been before. It was a bright, sunny morning as they drove along a deserted country road. It was a day where Emma just knew nothing could go wrong. And although it was a perfect day, and Emma knew she was going somewhere safe, she was still a little nervous to be going somewhere unfamiliar. She had never been to camp before, but was so happy to be going away from Dean.

When they arrived, Maureen parked the car on the gravel parking lot. She carried Emma's suitcase to the lobby of what looked like a big log cabin in the middle of the woods. Emma waited nervously while Maureen spoke with a woman who seemed to be in charge of the camp. The woman introduced herself to Emma and Maureen as one of the camp counselors. Within a few minutes, Maureen told Emma that she would be back in a week to pick her up and then she walked away.

For a moment, Emma watched as Maureen walked back into the sunlight, walked in the direction of her car. Then, Emma turned away and followed the camp counselor through the building. She was a very nice woman, younger than Maureen was, Emma guessed, dressed in a pair of casual shorts, camp t-shirt and tennis shoes.

Emma followed the counselor to a much larger cabin, not far from the main building, to one of the girls' cabins, where Emma would sleep for the week. The building consisted of bunk beds strewn about the entire space. It seemed as large as a barn, Emma thought, similar to the size of barn that her uncle from Arkansas, owned, with a giant-sized door. There were rows and rows of bunk beds, Emma noticed as she stopped with the counselor beside one of the bunks at the front of the building.

Girls Emma's age were leaning on or lying on bunk beds talking and laughing. Colorful dresses were hung on clothesline at the ends of the bunk beds. Emma noticed that most of the girls had five or six dresses hung on their bunks. The one dress she brought was going to seem out of place hanging at the end of her bed.

Church camp week was filled with sunshine and activities, including swimming at the camp swimming pool in the afternoons. Most of the girls knew how to swim, but there were a few girls, just like Emma, clinging to the side of the pool during afternoon swim time.

It seemed to Emma that most of the girls had arrived with several friends. There were few stragglers at camp, few girls ever apart from a small cluster of girls. Emma had arrived alone, and spent much of her time friendless while at camp. She watched the groups of girls, followed behind them on the way to activities during the day and in the evening, wishing she were part of one of the giggling groups. She considered that although she didn't have a single friend at camp, it was still better than being at the house on Third Street where her days were filled with hostility and violence. Alone was still lonely, but at least at camp it was safe to be alone, and Emma found peace within herself knowing that.

The week passed too quickly, and it was with a sick feeling in the pit of her stomach that Emma packed her suitcase. She wished someone could see into her tortured soul, know how awful her life was, and save her. Emma imagined that one of the adults at camp would walk up to her, perhaps the preacher, and lay their hand on her shoulder, and say, Emma, honey, we know what has been happening to you. You don't have to worry, be afraid or sad, anymore. We have decided that you should stay here. You shall live in one of the small cabins here on the church camp property.

Lost in her daydream of life away from Dean, a small smile tilted the corners of Emma's lips. Emma daydreamed about her future at the church camp—her new home—as she waited for Maureen in the big reception area where she had been dropped off a week ago. She hoped Maureen did not show up, and then she truly would have to live at the camp.

A cloud of dust swirled in the distance. A car driving up the gravel driveway disrupted Emma's daydream. As the car drew closer, Emma could see that it was Maureen's car. So much for her new home at camp, she thought as her heart and mood plummeted.

"How was camp?" Maureen asked, cheerfully.

"Fine," Emma mumbled as she climbed onto the passenger seat.

Emma was quiet during the drive home, and with each passing mile, her stomach grew sour.

To Emma's surprise, the rest of the summer was not *all* beatings, terror, nightmares and mysterious footsteps heard at night. A week after returning from camp, Maureen drove Emma to *her* special place, the town library. One hot August afternoon, Maureen and Emma walked side-by-side up the long sidewalk to the octagon shaped building that served as the town library. A wide sidewalk led to the concrete steps that wrapped around the front of the stone building. The library that had been built in the 1800's looked creepy and mysterious to Emma. She loved the mysterious feel of the building. Maureen walked Emma to the section of the library where she would find the books for her age group.

After the visit with Maureen, Emma was allowed to visit the library by herself, which she did, often. Sometimes Emma rode her green bike to the library, and other times she walked, pulling a wagon behind her to hold all the books she would read during the week. She couldn't carry all the books in her arms that the librarian allowed her to check out at one time. Even the wagon could not hold all the books she checked out, several toppling off the top and onto the ground on the five-block trip home.

The children's section of the library, in her opinion, was the most interesting section of the library. The room was circle shaped, not a typical square room. The library did not have air conditioning so the lights were never on during the day during the summer months due to the oppressive heat in the old building. A faint light glimmered through the windows set high above the bookshelves. Looking up toward the ceiling, Emma saw the soft light falling in a line, splashing on the wooden floor with small particulates of dust from the old books on the shelves dancing in the faint beams of light. For the rest of the summer, the library was Emma's quiet place; her safe place.

Emma spent hours flipping through the pages of old books. She would flip open the cover of books and read checkout dates. Many of the books had been stamped as checked-out 15 years ago. The librarian shared with her that her biological mother, Nancy, used to check out books from the library. She still had a library card on file. Nancy had checked out books from the same library, Emma mused. Perhaps she had stood in the same place by the librarian's desk, right where her feet were now. Her mother liked to read, or had at one time, Emma now knew, just like Maureen, she had liked to read. The library was a connection to a woman she had never known, a woman, she had been told, had died when she was a little girl.

13

The summer was almost over and in few weeks, Emma would be starting 6th grade. Before school started for the new year, Katie and Maureen both had birthdays to celebrate

Maureen's birthday was just a few days away and Amy had decided to do something special for her. While Maureen was out shopping on Saturday morning, Amy was going to bake a cake, and have it iced and waiting for her when she returned home. Emma was so excited. She knew Maureen would be happy with the fuss made over her birthday, something Dean never did.

The Saturday of Maureen's big day arrived and the oldest Snow girls were antsy for her to leave for a morning of grocery shopping and lunch. Finally, after Maureen provided instructions to the children, as if she were leaving for days instead of just a few hours, she drove down the street to the nearby town for her typical Saturday outing.

Amy darted through the living room, down the hall, and feet pounding on the wooden stairs, ran to the bedroom she shared with her three other sisters. Within minutes she was running back through the living room, a cake mix and icing in her hands, her destination, the kitchen.

Emma and Katie followed Amy to the kitchen to watch their sister make their mother's birthday cake. She looks like she knows what she's doing, Emma thought. Surprised, Emma watched as Amy mixed eggs, oil, mix, and water in a large bowl.

The aroma of the cake baking in the oven had Emma's mouth, watering. After baking for the directed amount of time, Amy took the cake out of the oven and placed it on the stove to cool. The cake did not look quite like the cakes Maureen baked. It was lopsided, but even lopsided, Emma was confident that Maureen would love the cake. Soon the cake was decorated with pink icing, and waiting for the birthday mom.

"Is she here yet?" Amy asked, excitedly.

"She just pulled up," Katie said, grinning.

Emma was in the living room sitting on the couch when Maureen walked through the door. She could feel the excitement in the house, Amy and Katie anticipating Maureen's happiness when she saw her birthday cake. Emma could barely contain herself; she was so excited to see the look on Maureen's face. She knew Maureen would gush over her cake!

Maureen did not disappoint the girls. The look of surprise and appreciation on Maureen's face when she walked into the kitchen and saw her special surprise was a wonderful gift to Amy.

The summer had not started well at all, but Emma thought, it had ended okay, and maybe it was a sign that sixth grade was going to be a super year.

The following weekend, on Saturday, the Snow girls spent the day with Maureen shopping for school clothes and school supplies. Emma was particularly fond of a blouse made of black fabric with tiny pink flowers with green leaves sprinkled on it. The blouse would match her new pink pants perfectly. Later that evening, Emma spread her new clothes across her bed, admiring her new tops and pants, deciding what she would wear on the first day of school.

14

The mornings and evenings were crisp, and the afternoons were still hot, and 6th grade was the *best* year of Emma's life. On the first day of school, Emma met the new girl, recognized her from church camp that she had attended that summer. Feeling uniquely brave, as if it were the year of change and possibility, Emma had approached the new girl as the rest of the class ran down the stairs to lunch, and introduced herself.

"Hi," Emma said, smiling at the brunet. "My name's Emma."

"Hi. I'm Callie," the new girl, said. She smiled a nice smile at Emma.

"Didn't you go to church camp this summer?" Emma asked, excited to have something in common with her potential new friend.

"Yeah!" Callie said.

"Me, too!" Emma said.

After that day, Emma and Callie were best friends, spending time after school and weekends at one another's homes. Callie lived near the baseball field at the edge of town in a trailer with her sisters and mom. Their home became Emma's second home, the one where an unkind word was never spoken and abuse was unheard of.

A book was propped on Emma's bent knees. It was a Nancy Drew book kind of day because Callie was spending the weekend with her dad. The two girls practically lived together, except when Callie had to visit her dad in the town where she used to live. Callie and her family had changed the horizon of Emma's world, providing a safe place where she could play, laugh, and not flinch every few minutes fearing she was about to be beaten. However, when Callie was gone to her dad's house, Emma was lonely, and switched to fear and isolation mode as she stayed out of Dean's way. She wished the weekends away during Callie's visitation weekends. Monday could not arrive fast enough for Emma.

Taking a break from reading her book, Emma thought about the conversation she and Callie had had during their walk home from school Friday. Although Halloween was weeks away, the girls were already planning their costumes. Of course, Callie and Emma would be trick-or-treating together. It was what best friends did. Maureen was great with costumes, able to pull an outfit together in minutes with whatever she found around the house. One year she had created a gypsy costume for Amy, using costume jewelry from her own jewelry box, and colorful sheer scarves, too.

Sunday, thank God, Emma thought. She sighed. Just one more day to get through, then she could be sitting in her favorite teacher's classroom, surrounded by friends. It had not been the greatest weekend. Dean had gotten in a few punches the night before when she walked through the living room to the kitchen, and earlier in the day he had grabbed her breasts and twisted them when she walked past him. Not only was she terrified of her dad, he made her skin crawl as if a thousand cockroaches were crawling on her. Emma shivered at the thought of cockroaches crawling on her and at the thought of Dean.

Emma walked into the living room and sensed that something was wrong. Maureen was rocking back and forth in her black rocking chair. She wasn't looking at anything or anyone. Her face looked strained, Emma thought, as if she were in pain. Emma looked over at the couch where Katie was sitting. She looked like she was feeling unwell, too.

Who died, Emma wondered uneasily, and walked to the kitchen to make a bowl of cold cereal.

Within an hour, Emma became aware of what had her stepmother looking as if she had lost her best friend.

Emma was sitting on the couch watching a movie when Maureen walked into the living room.

"Where's Amy?" Maureen demanded.

"I—don't know," Emma said.

"Amy!" Maureen shouted. She looked toward the kitchen and then the hall that led to the girl's bedroom.

"Go find her!" Maureen insisted.

Emma jumped up off the couch and rushed out of the room. She ran up the stairs toward her bedroom. It was there she found Amy.

"Maureen wants you. And I think she's mad about something," Emma said.

"Why?" Amy asked.

"I don't know," Emma said.

Amy had been sitting on the floor when Emma entered the room and now gracefully rose to her feet.

"Better hurry," Emma said, and followed her sister out the door and down the stairs.

Emma slowed her pace as she turned the corner in the hall. She watched as Amy walked away from the hall and entered the living room. From her vantage point in the hall, Emma could see Maureen standing in the center of the living room. She heard Maureen yelling, sounding like a crazed wild animal, or hurt animal, Emma thought. Scared, Emma stood still in the hall and listened.

"What have you done?" Maureen shrieked. "You tell me, right now! What is going on in this fucking house? What have you been doing with your father! Tell me!"

Emma gasped. Her heart thudded in her chest. Maureen was talking about the secret, about what Dean did to his children. She thought the adults, even Maureen, knew what he did. It wasn't as if it was a big secret. He was nasty, grabbing his girls little girl parts, not caring who was around, and the reason Amy had bed wetting issues, and Katie... it was what he did.

On her tiptoes, Emma walked to the living room. She stopped in the doorway.

Amy was standing several arm lengths away from Maureen, her face pale, eyes wide. Emma could see the tears glistening in her eyes, saw the tears trickle over her lashes and down her cheeks. Katie was sitting on the couch, looking down at the floor.

"What do you mean?" Amy asked, her voice barely a whisper. "Nothing is going on."

"I heard," Maureen said. "I heard what you have been doing with him. Everyone in town knows about it. Is it true, is it?" She was shouting now, and tears were rolling down her cheeks.

Tears burned Emma's eyes, and she felt the right side of her face begin to twitch. Her stomach rolled as if she were on a carnival ride at the county fair, as if she might throw up. It was then that it dawned on Emma that Maureen hadn't known. Emma had a spark of an idea. Maybe now that Maureen did know, she'd make Dean stop.

"Yes," Amy sobbed as tears continued to run down her cheeks.

Maureen screamed so loud Emma thought her ears would rupture.

"No. No. No. No," Maureen sobbed.

"I'm sorry," Amy whispered.

Maureen collapsed on the couch, leaned over and placed her head in her hands. Her long auburn hair created a veil and covered her face. Sniffling, she reached over and picked up the black telephone that was nearby on the side table.

Maureen dialed a number, waited a second and then began screaming into the handset at whoever had answered the phone at the other end.

"That son of a bitch," Maureen screamed into the telephone.

There was a pause, and then Maureen screamed, "Dean, your brother. He's been having sex with the girls!"

Maureen paused.

"With Amy!" Maureen screamed.

Emma watched as Maureen paused again, listening to her aunt, Marjorie.

"Did you *know* this was going on? Have you heard about this? Oh my, god! How can this be happening? Lying? Well I don't know. Why would little girls lie? They're not lying. Amy's not lying. I just know."

There was a long pause, and then Maureen, in a broken voice, said, "Okay." Maureen clattered the handset on its cradle and rested her head in her hands, again.

It seemed to Emma as if only a few minutes had passed before Dean's mom, Grandma Harriet, and his sister, Aunt Marjorie, rushed into the house.

Grandma Harriet walked to the kitchen, followed by Aunt Marjorie and Maureen. Emma watched the three women sit down at the table, Maureen taking Dean's place at the head of the table. Maureen was crying hysterically. Grandma Harriet's face was contorted in anger, and Aunt Marjorie was quiet, her face expressionless.

Emma sat curled on the couch. She clutched one of the small throw pillows to her chest as she watched the three ladies argue about her dad having sex with little girls.

Maureen screamed and cried as Grandma Harriet and Aunt Marjorie defended Dean. Grandma Harriet rose from her chair and walked to the cupboard and grabbed three white coffee cups. She filled the cups with black coffee, and then set a cup in front of Maureen and Marjorie. Emma smelled the coffee as the women sipped from their cups.

"You're being ridiculous!" Grandma Harriet said. Her upper lip curled in anger.

Aunt Marjorie nodded in agreement.

"What kind of children would say such lies about their dad? Fuckin' liars!" Grandma Harriet said, her voice sharp with anger.

"Why would they lie?" Maureen sobbed.

Maureen slammed her half-full coffee cup onto the table.

"Children don't lie about things like that!" Maureen insisted.

"Listen to yourself," Grandma Harriet said. "You go saying those things to people and they'll think you're crazy. Because it is crazy!"

Emma looked over at Katie and Amy, who were also on the couch watching and listening to the three women in the kitchen.

"Amy!" Maureen shouted. "Get in here!"

Emma watched her sister scoot off the couch, her fingers nervously fiddling the hem of her shirt, her face white as cotton, and smeared with tears. She watched as her sister stood, her shoulders slumped, and looked at the ground while she stood in front of the woman, as if in front of a firing squad.

The young girl stood in front of the women, and instead of receiving compassion, help, and a hero to save her day, she was beaten with their screams. She was called a liar because they did not want to know the truth, and she was called a horrible child because the truth was too painful and horrific to accept.

As Emma sat and watched her grandmother, aunt, and stepmother break her sister with the cruel words they lashed at her—broke her just as if they had picked her up and slammed her to the floor—she felt as if a part of her were dying.

Emma heard Deans booted feet clomp into the living room through side-door before she saw him. She looked over at him, and noticed as he walked across the room toward the kitchen, that he was not walking with his typical arrogance. His shoulders were stooped like a little boy who had just been caught being bad and knew he was in trouble.

He stopped when he got to the kitchen, his body half in the living room. Emma looked at his face, then at Amy's profile, and then glanced at the three women as they looked up at him.

Maureen pushed back her chair and got to her feet.

"Tell me—tell me if it's true! Have you been having sex with Amy?" Maureen demanded.

Dean's face turned grey. His mouth gaped open in surprise that those words had come out of her mouth. One of his secrets was being challenged, and by Maureen, of all people.

Emma looked at Amy who was standing next to the monster, Dean. Standing too close.

"She's lyin'," Grandma Harriet insisted. "You know she's always lookin' fer attention. She's doin' this fer attention."

Grandma Harriet glared at Amy.

"Why would she do that?" Maureen asked. "That's stupid. No little girl is going to lie about something like this. She doesn't even know what it means."

"Deanie! Deanie, you tell Maureen right now you didn't do what Amy's sayin'," Grandma Harriet insisted. "Tell 'er that child's just a lyin' little bitch. Go on now. Tell 'er. Well, tell 'er it's not true."

"I'd go to jail," Dean mumbled. "I'd go to jail. They'll take me to jail."

Dean looked around the room like a wild man. Then he looked at his mother.

"They'll take the girls away and I'll go to jail," Dean whined.

"You're not goin'' to jail," Grandma Harriet assured Dean. "She's just a lyin' kid. No one's gonna believe a word she says. And if Maureen says anything, they'll think she's crazy, too. People will think they're all crazy if they talk about it."

Grandma Harriet looked across the table at Maureen, and then glared at Amy.

Aunt Marjorie piped up in her childlike voice. "She's just a girl. Yuh can't believe anything she says, Deanie."

Emma could not believe her ears and eyes. Dean had said he'd *go to jail*, had just admitted to rape, so why, she wondered, was Grandma Harriet calling Amy a liar. The crazy on Third Street had just entered an entirely new and twisted dimension of crazy. She could not believe that Dean's mom was defending him. Grandma Harriet was defending his horribleness, and was not helping her granddaughter. Emma did not understand why. She felt cold and terrified as the minutes clicked away, as the adults tried to figure out how to best handle the newest family secret, how to continue hiding it.

So much for the after school specials, Emma thought, sarcastically. *Tell an adult if anyone touches you in the bad way, right. What a joke*! Emma continued to watch in disbelief as the adults screamed at Amy, trying to get her to say she had lied.

Amy's small shoulders shook as she stood in the kitchen, in front of Dean, Maureen, Grandma Harriet and Aunt Marjorie. Her long blonde hair, wet with tears, hung in her face. She cried in shame.

There would be no rescue, Emma realized. No one wanted to hear. There was no point in talking about what he was doing, had done, to her or any of the other girls in the house, because, Emma realized, they had known all along.

Family secrets, especially Dean's secret life of sexually assaulting his daughters, were going to remain in their house.

For now, Grandma needed to get Maureen calmed down. Dean, and Grandma Harriet could not have Maureen hysterical and telling the secret. Grandma Harriet tried to convince Maureen that the children were bad children, that it was not true, and that Dean's explanation that he would go to jail if anyone found out, was not an admission of guilt. He was confused, Grandma Harriet said as she wrapped her arm around Maureen's shoulder.

"He's just confused. It's quite the shock to be accused of raping a child," Grandma Harriet said, softly, and soothingly. "Now, we're all just going to forget about all this. These girls have issues. Let's all forget about this day. It's not true."

Emma watched Maureen, watched the emotions wash over her face, the confusion, the anger, and the fear. Emma had seen and heard a great deal of what happened in the house to her sisters. She knew, because it happened to her, too, and she knew in that moment, that Maureen knew it was true.

Maureen, quiet now, sat with her face resting on her hands and her shoulders slumped. She looked beaten to Emma. As Emma watched Maureen, she wondered if she was thinking about Laura, her little sister, Maureen's only daughter. Laura was a beautiful little girl, with soft brown curly hair that hung below her waist, only five years old. Was Maureen thinking of her now, what her husband—Dean—might do to her, or had already done to her? How would she ever be sure this would not, or had not happened to Laura?

It had scared Emma, watching Amy being beaten by her family, not beaten by their fists, as Emma was sometimes, but with the things they had shouted at her. Emma had learned as a toddler to be quiet, to be as invisible as she possibly could to avoid being beaten, and avoid what Amy had just experienced. But there was a difference between Emma and her brothers and sisters. For whatever reason, Dean singled Emma out, and beat her, on at least one occasion, almost to death. As she watched Amy and Maureen, Emma wondered how would it have been for her if it had been her standing in front of Maureen, Marjorie, Harriet and Dean instead of Amy. She was pretty sure it would have gone as her life usually did. They would have yelled at her, just as they had yelled at Amy, but she knew that it would have been more, so much more. She had to try harder to be invisible, to be quiet, to stay out of the way. Telling anyone that Dean had tried to kill her when she was a little girl, that he beat her, and touched her... she could not talk about it, not if she didn't want him to hurt her more than he was already was hurting her.

15

After the afternoon Grandma Harriet and Aunt Marjorie came to the house to talk to Maureen about Dean raping and sexually assaulting his daughters, the family never mentioned the secret again. The adults in the family allowed Dean to create opportunities to grope his daughters. They kept his children prisoners in his house, forcing them to fight Dean off as he tried to, and at times succeeded, in tearing their clothing from their bodies. They condoned the penetration of their bodies by their father, condoned his actions when he snuck into their beds at night while they were sleeping and assaulted them. They knowingly allowed Dean to rob them of their childhood years in all areas of the house, such as the bathroom, dirt-floored crawl space under the house, and even the shed behind the house. They sacrificed the Snow daughters to Dean for his sick, perverse sexual purposes.

It seemed to Emma that the truth spoken out loud had not mattered. Then, one day, after the first of the year arrived, during the last half of Emma's sixth grade year of school, her world completely fell apart.

Maureen packed Laura, Robby, and Timmy's things, and all of her belongings, which included dishes and furniture, and moved out. One Saturday morning she was there, and by the end of the day, she wasn't.

Emma knew why Maureen had left Katie, Amy and her behind in the house of horror. It was easier for Maureen to lie to herself, easier to believe that she hadn't been married to a man that preferred sex with little girls than with women. But it was true; Maureen was married to a child sexual predator. Believing a lie made it easier to turn her back and walk away, leaving innocent children in his care.

Maureen, Grandma Harriet or Aunt Marjorie could have called the police or a counselor at school, but they did not. And Maureen left quietly knowing in her gut what was going on, letting it continue.

Emma could understand that Maureen *had* to leave to protect her own children from Dean. Who in their right mind would stay in the house with a crazy person, with him? What she did not understand was how she could leave the other children with him so he could do all the things he was doing, as if it were okay. Emma was angry, disgusted, and scared.

Emma loved Maureen, the only mother she had ever known. She had not wanted her to leave, even though she knew that by leaving she was saving Laura, Timmy and Robby.

Emma saw Maureen in the house once after that day, when she stopped by for, Emma was not sure. One evening, while Emma was watching TV, while Dean was painting his bedroom, Maureen stopped by. Maureen and Dean walked to what used to be *their* bedroom, now empty but for a ladder, and a gallon of paint and paintbrush he was using to paint the room.

Emma looked to the left, toward Dean's bedroom, and saw Maureen with her arms wrapped around Dean's neck, and Dean's hands plastered on Maureen's butt. Rolling her eyes in disgust, Emma turned back to the TV.

The house on Third Street became very quiet with Maureen, Laura, Timmy and Robby gone. There were no more shopping trips or lunches with Maureen in town. And the bed Emma had shared with Laura seemed much bigger. During the dark of night, the sounds of footsteps were much louder, and she waited in terror for whatever or whoever made the sounds to reach out and get her, next.

Emma preferred the nights broken by Katie's irritated voice.

"Get off my side. Stop touching me," Katie hissed.

Amy and Katie's bed creaked as Katie climbed out of the bed.

Emma knew her sister's nightly ritual. Emma would lie on her bed, curled on her side and listen to Amy and Katie bicker back and forth because Amy had gotten too close to Katie. Then Emma would hear the creak of their bed as Katie climbed out of the bed. She could barely see Katie in the dark, but knew what she was doing. Katie had gotten out of bed, and stealthy as a ninja, was straightening her blanket in sleeping bag fashion. Emma would bet that even in the dark, Katie could pull her blankets tight enough so that if a coin were flipped on it, it would bounce in the air. Katie was very precise, very particular about her things. Although Emma could not see in the dark, she knew Katie's blanket was now wrinkle free, and folded in half, taking up exactly half of the bed. A portion of the blanket was pulled down, as if it were a sleeping bag, and Katie was slipping inside. And if Amy scooted too close to the wrinkle free side of the bed, Emma would know because she would hear Amy cry out *ouch* when Katie elbowed her in the side.

16

If Emma could, she would hide her changing body under baggy clothes, but Maureen was gone, so there was no one to buy her clothes. The clothes purchased by Maureen at the beginning of sixth grade year had all become too tight. Emma, a seventh grader, was five-foot-three, taller than her older sisters were, but her petite frame was frail in comparison to Dean. He was six-foot-one and almost two hundred pounds. Emma was curvier than Katie and Amy, her breasts, during puberty, seeming to grow a little larger each day, and Dean noticed. It was a challenge for Emma to avoid his prying hands and fingers when she walked through a room, so she tried to avoid him altogether. The only time Emma's body was safe from him was when her sisters and their friends were in the house.

One evening Dean arrived home from work and announced that he had a date. Emma was relieved to hear he was going out, and knew he was going on a date with his high school girlfriend who pretended, when she called the house, that she was an adult. Dean had been dating the high school girl since Maureen had left, and Emma suspected he had been dating her before Maureen had left him. Those were the best of evenings, in Emma's opinion, evenings when she could relax. The young girl was feeling pretty bold lately, calling the house frequently.

Emma would answer the phone to a husky girl's voice asking, "Is your dad home?" Emma would ask, although she knew who it was, "May I ask who's calling?" And the young girl trying to fake being an adult, would respond, "It's Ruth."

Emma, Katie and Amy would get a chuckle out of the girl on the line, and try to guess which junior or senior at Katie's school was screwed up enough to date a child predator. Katie, Amy and Emma were not supposed to know that Dean was dating someone under age, but they knew. It baffled them how he managed to get away with the sick things he did, like grooming and sexually abusing one of the girls in the local high school. It was so easy for him, to rape young girls, because no one in town seemed to care about such things.

When Dean prepared for an evening out with his high school girlfriend, he was always as giddy, and goofy acting as the boys in Emma's junior high. And Emma was safe, for the evening.

Katie and her friend, Kim, had stopped by the house to pick something up before heading to Kim's house for the night. Emma liked Kim, and liked it when she came to the house. When Kim came to the house, and Dean was there, he forgot about Emma, which meant a grope and beating-free evening for Emma. But the situation made Emma uncomfortable because it felt as if Kim was a sexual assault replacement. If he was assaulting someone else, such as Kim, that meant Dean left Emma alone. She felt guilty, but also relieved at the reprieve.

Kim and Emma were laughing about some silly thing Kim had shared, when Dean walked into the house, surprising Emma. She thought he had already left for the evening with his girlfriend.

"Hey, Kim," Dean said as he walked into the living room.

Emma stepped back several steps from Kim and watched the interaction between Dean and Katie's sixteen-year-old friend.

"Hey, Deanie!" Kim said, and grinned up at him. "What are you doing home? I'd think you'd have a date with some cute lady."

Dean loved the attention Kim showered on him.

"Well, how 'bout you," he said. "Don't you have a date tonight with some cute guy?"

Kim threw her head back and laughed.

"You are so full of shit!" Kim, laughed.

Kim punched his shoulder, and Dean responded by wrapping his arm around her neck in a headlock.

Kim screamed, but Emma could see that there was a grin on her face.

Dean wrestled Kim to the ground, and for several minutes, they writhed around on the linoleum floor. Rolling her over, Dean climbed on top of Kim, pinning her wrists to the floor. Kim shrieked when he began tickling her stomach. He let her up, and Kim ran out of the room, into the hall that led to the girls' bedroom upstairs.

Since becoming best friends with Callie, Emma had spent as many nights as possible with her friend, and if not at Callie's house, then Callie spent the night at Emma's house with her. It was another way to guarantee safe nights. Dean did not touch or beat Emma when Callie was around.

Tonight Amy and Katie were gone, spending the night at a friend's house. Emma's plan was to spend the night with Callie, but Dean had rained on that plan. He wanted her home for some stupid reason, Emma thought, grumpily.

It was dark outside, and Emma was alone in the house. She had come home from school hours earlier to an empty house. It was light when she had gotten home. There had been a soft glow made by the sunlight in the living room. Emma didn't mind being home alone in the big house when it was light out. It was when it got dark outside that she became afraid. The shadows in the corners of the rooms grew longer and darker, especially in the hallway leading to her bedroom. The house changed when it got dark. It felt as if *things* were in those shadows, watching her. She knew there was nothing in the dark, but she could never quite talk herself out of the fear. Maybe she was afraid because for so many years Dean, her sisters and Maureen would wait inside the dark house after they had all been outside playing. Emma would be the last one to come inside the house. She would walk around the house, in the dark, and then walk up the stairs of the porch, the screen door slamming behind her, and enter the dark living room.

"Hello," she would call out. "Where is everyone?"

Then the family would jump from behind furniture at her, screaming scary sounds.

It might not be too bad tonight, Emma considered. It was late enough now that surely Dean was hanging out with his girlfriend, the mysterious, Ruth.

Emma was taking a break from watching a sitcom. She was in the kitchen placing frozen pizza on a pizza pan—typically the only food that was ever in the house—when she heard the side door to the porch slam shut. The slamming door startled her.

Pausing in the pizza preparations, Emma held her breath waiting for Amy or Katie to enter the kitchen. Her heart plummeted when she realized the luck fairy hadn't decided to pay her a visit when *he* walked into the kitchen.

Emma glanced at Dean's face, assessing his mood. He seemed to be in an okay mood, she considered. There was no sign of darkness that would indicate her head was going to be bashed into a wall. The tone of the evening changed in an instant, going from peace and safety to a feeling of uneasiness and watchfulness.

Emma took the pizza out of the oven and placed it on the kitchen table on top of a hot pad. She stuffed the sigh deep within, hid the fear she felt, and willed her hands to be steady as she cut the pizza into slices. Emma turned toward the cabinet to get a plate for her pizza, but *he* had beaten her to it.

Dean was standing next to her with a plate in each of his hands, one for Emma and one for himself.

I guess he is having pizza, too, Emma thought, uncomfortably. She didn't know what to make of his human gesture, handing her a plate.

Emma always avoided Dean, *always* made it a point never to willingly be alone in a room with him. Now she was trapped. Out of the corner of her eye, Emma saw Dean staring down at her, noticed the strange look on his face.

"Are you going out tonight, with Ruth?" Emma asked. As she waited for his answer, Emma held her breath.

"No," Dean said. "I'm gonna stay in tonight."

Suddenly, Emma wasn't hungry anymore. She felt downright sick. How was she going to make it through the evening alone with him, she worried. Her sisters wouldn't be home to save her. No Kim. And he didn't have a date. Stuck. She began to panic.

It wouldn't have been so bad if he would have at least had a date tonight. Then he would have gotten home late, tired. He would have been in a good mood after seeing the mysterious Ruth. Emma didn't want to stay downstairs with him, but didn't want to go to her room either because he would follow her. She tried to think of the safest possible plan.

Years of polishing the art of avoidance had given her an idea of the safe zones in the house. Bedrooms and dark places were not safe, but the living room was typically safe, but of course, that was because usually there were more people in the living room. Right now, it was just the rapist, and Emma. She began to sweat from nervousness. She never knew what to say to him, so rarely did she speak to him. He probably believed that she had long since lost her ability to speak. Invisibility was another art Emma was perfecting. She was learning to blend in with her surroundings, never standing out, and becoming one with the wallpaper or newly painted walls.

Dean and Emma ate their pizza in the kitchen as they sat at the table, in silence. Emma ate quickly, ripping off huge chunks and barely chewing before swallowing. After they were done eating, Emma washed the dishes while Dean sat on the new couch that Ruth had helped him pick out. Maureen had taken most of the furniture with her when she moved out. Most of the furniture had been hers, except the old beds in Emma's bedroom that had belonged to the dead couple that used to live in the house. The new couch had been a surprise when Dean brought it home. It was very modern and not Dean's old-timer country-style at all.

Emma drug out washing dishes as long as she could. She was sure all the dishes were squeaky clean. No chance he would find a tid-bit of food clinging to a dish tonight, Emma thought, and not likely that he would be dragging her butt out of bed at three in the morning to wash all of the dishes in the cabinets.

His military training, during his very short stint in the military, had really paid off, Emma thought with a roll of her eyes. She knew he fancied himself a powerful drill sergeant, pulling his recruits out of bed in the middle of the night, shouting orders at them to wash the dishes, shine their shoes and do pushups all with the intention that these military men must be prepared just in case they were captured by the enemy. Creating superior minds through sleep deprivation was their goal, just as it was Dean's goal for his girls. Except that Emma was not a drafted army man and there was no chance of being captured by the enemy because she was currently residing with him.

Sleep disrupted nights were awful during the school year. When she was finally allowed to go back to bed, sleep came immediately, but moments later, at least it felt that way, the alarm would begin to blare. The next morning her face would be puffy and she would have a glazed look about her for the entire day. Many of Emma's school days were spent in a daze because she was either woken by Dean in the middle of the night to perform some household chore or she was afraid to fall asleep, afraid she'd be woken by Dean groping her body. The result was the same, the next day she was so tired that she would walk around like one of the undead. And the footsteps during the night woke her up, and then kept her awake.

After Emma hung the dishtowel up, she walked into the living room, intent on walking to her bedroom.

"Here," Dean said, in an oddly whiny voice.

Oh crap, Emma thought as she turned toward his voice. Dean was lying on his side, propped on an elbow, on the couch. He scooted his body back towards the backrest of the couch, creating more room for Emma to lie beside him.

"Lay down next to me," Dean said. He patted the empty space on the couch in front of him.

Shiiiitt, Emma said to herself. What to do, she thought frantically. Bolt out of the house, feign a headache like women did in made for TV movies, or . . . or. There was no or to it. Emma had to walk over to the couch and lay down next to him. There was nowhere to run. As she continued to stare at Dean, she wondered if other girls were as horrified to lie next to their dad's as she was, and if any of them ever did lie next to their dad's. She doubted it.

"Come on," Dean said.

He did not shout the words at her, and did not rip his belt off and threaten to beat her. But at that moment, Emma saw something in his eyes, and she sensed that the situation was even more dangerous than any of the times that he had beaten her or sexually assaulted her. It was a feeling she had that if she did not walk over to him, something horrible would happen to her and if she *did* walk over to him, something horrible was going to happen to her.

"Emma," Dean said. He patted the couch.

Emma couldn't breathe as she crossed the room. She stood for a moment and looked down at Dean who was looking up at her. He was wearing jeans, his giant jingly wad of keys attached to his belt thingy. He had taken off his button-up shirt and was now wearing a short-sleeved t-shirt. He stunk of the Old Spice aftershave he had splashed on earlier, bathed in it was more like it, Emma thought with revulsion. Did he really think his teeny-bopper girlfriend liked that crap, she wondered. The turquoise on his bracelet caught her eye when he patted the couch, again.

Where the hell was Jesus, Emma wondered, angrily.

She turned in a half circle, and primly, Emma sat down on the edge of the couch, her legs pressed tightly together.

Dean tugged at her to lay down.

Stiffly, in one motion, Emma swung her legs up and onto the couch, keeping her thighs pressed tight together, and forced her body down onto the firm surface of the couch. She lay her head on her out-stretched arm and tried to focus on the figures on the TV.

Dean draped his arm over Emma's waist, and let it rest there for a moment.

Emma held her breath, her body as stiff as one of Dean's two-by-fours. Her skin crawled where he touched her. She felt Dean stir behind her, pressing closer into her. He flung a heavy leg over her legs, holding her in place. His arm slid from her waist to her hip. Emma squirmed as she tried to free her legs from beneath his heavy leg. He wrapped his leg tighter and pulled her closer. She braced her right hand on the couch and pulled her body forward, but could not budge even an inch. He was too heavy and too strong for her to get away.

Her most primal instincts took over and Emma began to struggle as if her life depended on it, to be free from the couch and from the weight of Dean's body. She felt as if she was suffocating, felt pressure on her ribs, and then on a breast. She clenched her fists and ground her teeth, and pulled forward. As Emma struggled, she felt Dean slide his hand inside the front of her jeans, inside her underwear. Her dad's hand violated her most private part.

The next morning, Emma woke up alone in her bedroom. Her sisters were not home yet. The house was quiet, and felt empty. Dean must have gone to the restaurant where his girlfriend worked, Emma thought. Relieved, she flopped onto her other side, and pulled her blanket closer to her throat. Eventually, nature dictated that she get out of bed. She walked down the creaky old staircase and into the living room on her way to the bathroom.

Alone in the house, as if the night before had not happened, Emma spent several hours doing what other kids her age did, she watched Saturday morning cartoons.

17

Emma's life sunk to a new level of hell. Her sisters were hardly ever home anymore, which left her home alone with Dean more often. Emma was constantly walking on eggshells, trying not to ignite Dean's dark moods where he would snap and beat her. Now that she was older, the beatings with objects had ceased. And now that Katie and Amy were hardly ever home, and Maureen and her other siblings no longer lived in the house on Third Street, Dean did not have an audience, so there was no need to have Emma strip naked for beatings. Now, Dean's beatings consisted of punching Emma about the face and head as if they were in a boxing ring, or twining her long hair around his fingers and his hand, and bashing her head into a wall. No audience required. But there were other forms of torture, the never knowing when Dean would touch her, and when she woke to find him touching her.

    The sound of the end of the school day bell brought with it dread for Emma because it meant it was time to walk or ride her bike the five blocks to her house. She never knew if Dean would be home during the evening or if he would be out with his teenaged girlfriend, Ruth.
    The loud bell echoed in the old building. Kids jumped up out of their chairs and ran out of the classroom on to what Emma was sure would be a wonderful beginning to their evenings. Emma rose slowly

from her chair and shuffled to the door not in any particular hurry to go anywhere as she had nowhere wonderful to go. She did not know what the evening or night had in store for her at the house of horrors.

No friend accompanied her on her walk to her red ten-speed bike. Callie had to do something with her family tonight. Emma was on her own. No Callie to protect her tonight, as she had on so many other nights. The schoolyard was almost empty as Emma took her time walking to her bike. Still stalling, she sat on the seat and kicked the stand with her foot taking her time to look around at the other straggling kids in the yard. Sighing, Emma pushed off with her foot, and began the ride to Third Street.

The house was quiet when Emma pedaled into the yard. She walked up the concrete steps that Dean had put in the year before, opened the screen door, and walked into the darkened, deserted living room. First stop was the kitchen to search for a snack. Since Maureen had left, the kitchen was usually pretty bare. Last summer, Emma had her first summer job, babysitting for a family in town. The money had been put to good use, buying food, since Dean had not caught onto the concept that he was now responsible for providing food for his daughters. And she had earned a little extra money from Johnny, her Grandma Harriet's ex-husband, too.

When Emma's aunt and uncle's house had burned down, the family had asked Emma and her sisters if they wanted to earn a little money by helping Johnny go through and clean up the house. Emma had been happy to earn some cash, and had agreed. It was the first house she had ever been inside of after it had been on fire. It was the strangest thing walking through a house where she had spent a great deal of time throughout her young life. The walls were almost completely gone, just fire blackened and burned wood. She could see into the rooms before entering, because the walls no longer existed. The girl's room, where her cousins slept and kept all their things, had shoes clumped together in piles, and other things that would never be taken to their new house. Things damaged, and never to be used again. Emma's job had been to sweep all the ruined things into piles and then Johnny would go through it later. She assumed he would load it all in a truck and take it to the dump.

One night, the last night working for Johnny, he had asked her for a hug before she left. Although he was technically a grandfather type person, had been married to her grandmother, he made her a little uncomfortable, but then, most men did make her a little uneasy.

"Emma," Johnny said, "how 'bout a hug for your old grandpa before you go home?"

Emma was standing in what at one time had been the living room of her aunt and uncle's home. It was dark, just a glow of light from a work light cut into shadows of the room. She had just walked out of one of the bedrooms and was on her way to the back door, the door she had walked through hundreds of times. She would walk out the door, down the steps, down the alley to her house.

Emma looked at Johnny. The light was behind him, casting his face in shadow. He should be harmless enough, she told herself as she watched him wipe his hands on an old rag.

Slowly, she walked toward him. She stopped in front of him, and looked up at him.

Johnny placed his hands on her shoulders and pulled her into him.

She placed her hands on his arms, in a half-hearted hug.

His arms around her waist, he pulled her tight to him, and then grasped her arms, pulling them up toward his neck. He unfolded her hands, and rested them on his shoulders.

His hands moved back to her waist, and then slid lower to her bottom, pulling her into him. His hands squeezed, just as she had seen Dean to Maureen.

Emma pulled away and before he could grab her, she ran to the door. She ran through the yard, down the alley and up the steps to the side entry of the house on Third Street.

The next afternoon, Dean told her that Johnny wanted to know what time she was going to be there to help clean, and she mumbled that she was not going back. Emma had thought Dean would force her to go back to help clean because it was good money, and had been surprised when he had not said one word to her, just looked at her.

Dean always had the things he wanted to eat as snacks and for his work lunches. The girls knew better than to touch his food. Amy and Katie ate at their friend's houses quite often, and Emma was thankful that she had had a babysitting job so she could buy a sandwich for dinner or a late lunch each day.

Emma sat on the couch watching TV, enjoying the peace and quiet of being home alone, still not sure what the evening would hold for her. It wasn't long before Katie and Kim showed up at the house. Emma assumed Katie must have come home to get some clothes or books, and would be off to Kim's house for the night, as usual. Kim was funny. It was like watching a funny sitcom when she was around, always laughing and screeching about something.

If Dean happened to come home, Emma hoped Kim would be there.

About a half an hour later, Amy walked into the living room. It was rare that both Katie and Amy were in the house at the same time.

This was a good situation, Emma thought, relieved not to be home alone. She would not have to be home alone with Dean.

Dean arrived around six and in a good mood. Emma knew his *good* mood was because he had seen Kim's car parked in front of the house. He walked into the living room with a grin on his face, looking for Kim. She squealed when she saw him. It was a loud evening with all the Kim noise and no one noticing Emma, which was always her objective.

Dean and Kim played around for a while. Eventually, he jumped to his feet and announced that he had to get going because he had a date. It was getting late so when he announced that he was going out, Emma was surprised, but happy with the news.

At about nine, when Dean was in the bathtub, Kim said her goodbyes and headed to her house.

It was as if when Kim walked out the door, out of the house, she took the noise and energy with her. Except for the TV, it was quiet in the living room. It was an uncommon type of evening spent watching TV with her sisters, just as they had done so many times before when they were little girls.

A short while later, Dean opened the door to the bathroom, and a towel draped around his waist, walked through the living room, continuing onto his bedroom. Thank God, there had been no calls for one of them to help him with his bath, Emma thought as she wrinkled her nose. That was absolutely not what little girls should have to do, help their dad take a bath. On occasion, Dean had called Emma into the bathroom to help him scrub up. When she walked into the bathroom, she'd find him scrubbing away at his arms and legs with a brush that was used to clean dishes with; scrubbing at his skin so hard it was red. It seemed to Emma, the way he was digging at his skin, he must have felt awfully dirty. The occasions when Dean called Emma into the bathroom to help with his bath, it was always date night. He could scrub as hard as he wanted, Emma thought, but he would never be able to scrub what he had done to his daughters, never be able to clean the filth, from his soul. As Emma scrubbed Dean, she stared at the wall. He would yell at her that she was missing spots on his body. He insisted that she pay attention and look at what she was doing, the image of every part of Dean's body seared in her memory forever.

Emma was relieved when Dean walked into his bedroom, and then closed the door behind him and a few minutes later he walked back into the living room, wearing different clothes.

"Girls," Dean said as he buckled his belt, "I wanna show you something." He turned away and walked back toward his bedroom.

Katie, Amy and Emma looked at each other, wondering what their deranged dad wanted.

"Come on," Dean said, standing in the doorway of his bedroom.

Emma followed behind Katie and Amy, toward a room she really did not want to go into. The girls lined up as if in a firing squad, shoulder-to-shoulder, beside Dean's bed. The bed was neatly made, Emma noticed. Her anxiety skipped to high alert when she saw all the guns, in varying sizes, that were on the bed. A quick count tallied almost eight handguns. And why, Emma wondered nervously, was Dean needing to show them guns.

Dean walked around the other side of the bed as if he were in some sort of strange classroom, he the teacher and his daughters his students. He picked up each gun, one by one, held it in his hand, cocked it, making clicking noises that made Emma jump. The guns were in varying sizes, one small enough to hide in his hand which he demonstrated.

As Emma watched Dean demonstrate each one of the guns, a scary revelation washed over her. If Dean wanted to, he could do quick and permanent damage to her and her sisters. She knew Dean did not allow his children in his bedroom and he rarely talked to them. He was a crazy man, and crazy man was sending them a message which was that if they stepped out of line in any way, he would do more than bash their head against a wall, he'd shoot them. Emma looked at Katie and Amy to see their reaction to the guns, and saw the fear on their faces, knowing they had gotten his message, too.

Dean squeezed past the girls as they waited to be dismissed, and with his back toward them, as the girls looked at each other, he placed the guns in a closet near the door of his bedroom.

"Out," Dean said and brushed his arm toward the door of his bedroom. The demonstration was over, Emma thought with relief.

After Dean had left for his date, Katie, Amy and Emma remained rooted to their spots in the living room. The noise from the TV was a hum, just background noise.

"Well," Katie said. "I guess he's going to shoot us."

Amy and Emma stared at Katie and nodded their heads in agreement.

All of a sudden, Emma felt exhausted. It had been a safe evening with Kim and Emma's sisters in the house, aside from the very bizarre and scary gun demonstration portion of the evening. Now, she just wanted to shut her eyes to her world and let sleep take her. She climbed the 13 stairs in the dark hall that led to her bedroom. Dean would not be home for hours, Emma suspected, which meant she should get a few hours of much needed sleep.

When Emma walked into her black as ink room, she swung her arms around until she felt the string that was tied to the light bulb hanging from the ceiling. She had to wait until the string swung back by her hand and then strategically snatched it, pulling in one motion. Bright light spilled into the room. She found an over-sized t-shirt to wear to bed and pulled it over her head. There was a chill in the room and Emma rubbed her arms. Dean had said he was going to fix up her bedroom as he had the rest of the house, but until then there was no heat in the room. It was cold during the fall and winter months, and the girls dripped with sweat during the summer.

Emma climbed into bed and snuggled under the one thin blanket she had. She lay her head on the old flat pillow and closed her eyes, leaving the light on for her sisters.

Something didn't feel right. Her eyes popped open. She felt uneasy. Sighing, she thought, this is ridiculous. It had been a very nice evening and she knew she should be feeling relaxed but instead she felt scared. She could not shoo the feeling away.

Emma climbed back out of bed, the cold air in the room wrapping around her causing her to shiver. She walked to the closet in the corner of the room and moved clothes back and forth. When her fingers touched something soft and furry, she tugged and it fell into her hands. She pulled on the too-small winter coat, and crawled back into bed.

Emma hoped Katie and Emma would not notice that she was wearing a winter coat to bed. That would be fodder for older sisters to tease the younger sister. Emma rolled over onto her side, her back to Katie and Amy's bed, her face toward the purple colored wall that Maureen had painted before she moved out.

Emma closed her eyes and drifted off to sleep. It seemed like only moments later that Emma blinked her eyes, seeing only darkness. She felt her bed move up and down. Sucking in her breath, she realized that someone was in bed next to her, and that someone was much larger than her sisters were. Whoever was in bed with her, scooted closer to her. She felt a hand on her waist. She had forgotten about the furry winter coat she had put on before getting into bed and now the hand rubbed the soft fabric.

"What the hell you wearin'? A coat?" Dean asked, angrily.

Dean had crawled into bed with Emma while she slept, and while Katie and Amy slept in their bed in the same room. Emma's sleep-groggy brain was having difficulty catching up to the situation. He was angry that Emma was wearing a coat in bed, frustrated that instead of her skin beneath his hand, he felt the fur of a coat.

What was he going to do to her, Emma wondered as she began to panic. Dean was obviously angry, was pushing at her, hurting her as he dug his fingers into her side. She closed her eyes tight, steeling herself from the punches she expected to land about her body.

She felt his legs spooned next to her body, but his upper torso was upright as he looked down at his daughter.

"I-I was cold," Emma stammered.

Icy pellets of fear slid down the center of Emma's back.

Dean pushed roughly against Emma, and then she felt the bed shift and the floor creaked with his weight as he stood up and walked out of the room.

Emma's heart was pounding. She continued to lie on her side, not daring to move.

Katie and Amy were home *and* in the same room with Emma, lying right across the room from her in their bed. Fear grabbed Emma's heart and squeezed as she realized that she was not safe from Dean, even when her sisters were in the same room.

18

Emma was stuck at home again, but tonight Amy was stuck with her. The two girls were in their bedroom avoiding Dean who was in the room below lying on the couch and watching TV. Emma watched Amy stand by the small closet in the corner of the room looking for something to wear to school the next day.

Crash!

Amy turned toward Emma, and with her eyes wide with terror, stared at her.

Emma jumped up off the bed where she had been lying, and rushed over to where Amy was standing. They looked down at the closet floor where a mound of clothes was now lying, the current rod mixed in with the mess.

Oh no, Emma thought. She looked into Amy's eyes. Both girls knew that Dean would have heard the crashing sound of the clothes and rod falling and would be on his way that very second to their bedroom. Amy and Emma had done their best to avoid Dean that evening, and they had almost made it. It was almost time to crawl under their covers and go to sleep.

Emma heard the sound of heavy work boots pounding on the old wooden stairs in the hall. The door slammed open, hitting the wall. The girls turned toward the man standing in the entryway, one hand on the doorknob and the other hand on his waste.

"What the hell was that?" Dean demanded to know.

Dean walked over to where Emma and Amy were standing, and stared down at the pile of clothes lying on the closet floor. It did not take much to push Dean into a rage, and this, Emma thought, was clearly something. Emma knew she was in for it. She held her breath and waited for the fist that would reach out and hit her, or the hand that would grab her hair and begin pounding her head into the wall. The nerve endings on her shoulders screamed as she waited.

Hunching her shoulders, Emma looked out of the corner of her eye. He was just standing there staring at the floor.

"Let's get this cleaned up," Dean said.

Emma turned her head and looked directly at Dean's face. He seemed okay, she considered.

Emma looked at Amy, and Amy looked at Emma. Leary of what Dean was up too, Emma leaned over and picked a top off of the pile of clothes that reached mid-thigh. Dean walked over to the bed and stood, watching as Amy and Emma carried armfuls of clothes to the bed.

Sometime during the closet cleanup process, Emma became aware that Amy had stopped helping. Looking across the room, Emma saw Amy and Dean lying on their sides on the bed, in spooning position. Dean and Amy stared at Emma as she looked back at them as she hung a top on a wire hanger.

Emma reached into the closet and slid the hanger on the rod that Dean had hung. Footsteps. Emma would have sworn she heard the footsteps she sometimes heard at night when she was in bed. Her hand was still on the hanger as she listened. Slowly, Emma withdrew her hand and stepped out of the closet, still looking up at the curtain rod, now holding several tops and a pair of pants. She looked to the left, toward the bed. Amy and Dean were still lying on the bed in the same position, with clothes draped over them. The sound of footsteps continued in a slow rhythmic pace.

Wrinkling her brow, Emma considered that something was not right. She could see Amy; they were in the same room, so she had to be safe, but her gut told her that something was very, very wrong. Every few minutes Emma glanced over at the bed as she continued to sort through the clothes on the floor. At one point, Emma paused, her body stiff as a thought occurred to her, a thought so horrific that she shook her head, trying to shake away the thought. He wouldn't rape one of her sisters with her in the same room, or would he, she wondered. He had tried to rape her with Amy and Katie in this very room, so why not? *That* was the something that had not felt right. That was why he had not exploded in rage when he saw the mess on the closet floor. Dean had created a humiliating, horrific rape opportunity.

Emma noticed the room had grown quiet. The footsteps had stopped. She looked around the room. Dean walked out of the room and Amy was curled up at the head of her bed.

It took about an hour to sort through the clothes and hang them back on hangers, and then hang the clothes back in the closet. When Emma was done, she stood in the center of her bedroom and stared at Amy. It felt as if a heavy weight was pressing down on her. Emma reached up to the string hanging from the ceiling, and pulled, washing the room in darkness.

19

Eighth grade, like her life, sucked, Emma reflected as she stared at the over-flowing garbage can. Amy, Emma thought angrily, why aren't you home to take out the garbage, after all it is *your* job. Amy and Katie were gone for the night again, which left Emma stuck with Amy's garbage chore. Dean was in the garage working on one of his fixer-upper cars.

  Emma rolled her eyes and thrust her hands on her hips, and thought, well, I might as well get the garbage out before ding-dong comes in and finds me standing around. Sighing heavily, she bent forward and grabbed the garbage-dirtied plastic can and lifted, at least, she tried to lift. She changed the position of her fingers, sticking them under the rim of the can and wrestled it across the newly carpeted floor. When she arrived at the door to the laundry room, she stood up and rubbed the pain from her fingers. She opened the door wide and pulled the garbage can into the small laundry room, and then pulled the kitchen door closed. As she walked into the garage, Emma glanced over at Dean, his back to her as he worked on something under the hood of a car. She walked through the garage and continued onto the side of the house, back behind a shelter of bushes where the burn barrel was placed. Hoisting the can up and over the rusted burn barrel, Emma emptied the contents. After wasting several matches trying to light the garbage on fire, it finally caught.

When Emma walked through the garage, she glanced over at the car where Dean had been standing when she had walked through the first time. Dean was no longer standing in front of the car. She looked around the rest of the large room. The garage was empty, no Dean. As she walked up the steps and into the laundry room, she wondered where he had gone. Emma had hoped Dean would remain in the garage all evening away from her.

When she opened the door to the kitchen, she found him. Dean was standing in the center of the room with his hands on his hips, waiting for her. Emma did not have time to shut the door, did not have time to walk across the room to place the garbage can by the window.

Dean grabbed Emma's arm just above her elbow, and forced her to her knees.

"Look at that," Dean, demanded. He pressed Emma's cheek against a cabinet.

"Do yuh see it? A scratch. God, you're fuckin' clumsy!" Dean shouted.

Twisting his fingers through Emma's hair, Dean pulled her head back and then slammed her face into the side of the cabinet.

Emma fell forward onto her hands when Dean released his hold on her hair.

A tiny scratch, Emma had seen the faint line of a scratch in the wooden drawer of the cabinet. *Shit!* A scratch on his dear cabinet was indeed a serious offense. How in the world had he known the scratch was there, she wondered, and why did he think she was responsible for the scratch.

Emma was well aware that Dean was not a rational human being, and typically, he did not try to rationalize beating her up. Now, on her hands and knees in front of him, she knew he was exerting power of releasing his crazy anger at her for something someone else had done to him. Dean, Emma knew, was nuttier than a Christmas fruitcake.

Dean grabbed Emma by the arm and yanked her to her feet. He wrapped his fingers through her long hair, again pulling his hand tight against her head.

Fearing Dean would rip out a handful of her hair, Emma reached her right hand up to her head and grabbed her hair close to her scalp. When Dean jerked his arm back, her hair still tangled through his fingers and hand, Emma lost her balance and stepped backward. The white wall came toward Emma at a dizzying speed when Dean slammed her head against the hard surface.

The room seemed overly bright to Emma. She clung to her head with her right hand, and flung her left hand out in front of her, trying to grab onto something. Emma's wire-rimmed glasses dug into her nose and the side of her face before they flew off, landing somewhere on the floor. Emma lurched forward as Dean pulled his arm back, and then forward again, slamming her head in to the wall a second time. When he ripped his fingers out of her hair, releasing her, she lost her balance and stumbled forward. She caught herself before she fell to the floor, having no intention of giving him the satisfaction of dropping her to her knees a second time.

Emma did not see Dean leave the room, but heard the door slam. She steadied herself for a moment, stood still until the dizziness subsided. The room was fuzzy. She needed to find where her glasses had fallen. Glancing toward the door, she saw only white, no fuzzy outline of a body and knew Dean had gone back to the garage. Kneeling down, Emma ran her hand in a sweeping motion over the kitchen carpet. Crawling forward, she continued the sweeping motion with her hand until her fingers felt the metal frame of her glasses.

Placing them on her nose and ears, Emma assessed the damage. The frames were bent pretty badly, now sitting tilted on her face. A few bends and adjustments later, and they fit a little better on her face. She sighed as she got to her feet, thinking that her glasses had certainly suffered right along with her face at the expense of Dean's fists.

Next, she picked up the garbage can that was lying on its side and placed it by the window. Emma stood for a moment by the window and looked across the empty lot. She wanted to fall to her knees and cry, but what would be the point, and besides, she was too tired to cry.

20

Fall gave way to the harshness of winter. Emma did not really like winter. It seemed like a sad time to her. All the trees and plants looked dead, and the cold, gloomy season brought out the ugly in people. Maybe it was because everyone was stuck inside together because it was too cold and nasty to be outside for very long, or maybe it was because of the dark grey days of winter. Winter was a particularly strange time at the house on Third Street. Emma's winter routine consisted of spending a great deal of time at home alone with Dean. She suspected the reason Dean was home so often lately was that his little girlfriend had broken up with him. He needed to get back out there, Emma thought with disgust, back in the dating world to find someone other than his daughters to grope.

Most evenings brought battles of fighting off Dean. Emma lived in a constant state of fear, even cracking open a book to avoid her life was impossible because she had to stay aware. Getting lost in a book could allow the creep to catch her unawares. She had to remain alert.

It amazed Emma that Dean believed he could do with her what he wanted, as if her body was not her own, but instead, his. Emma was a tangled mess of emotions, terrified of Dean, and angry with her sisters because they were never home. It all seemed so hopeless to her.

When Emma was a little girl, Christmas had seemed so magical. It had been the one time of the year when wishes were more likely to be granted by Jesus Christ, a time when people just seemed nicer. And even though Dean did not let a little thing like the birth of Jesus deter him from beating Emma, the hope of Christmas seemed to make life better. But as the years passed, even Christmas—the reminder of Jesus—were not inspiring a great deal of hope in Emma.

December had arrived at the house on Third Street, and this year Dean had actually bought a tree. There were even presents under the tree.

Katie and Amy were home on Sunday afternoon, Amy sitting in the living room while she talked to a friend on the telephone, and Katie was cooking something in the kitchen. Emma was lying on an old mattress in the room off the hall. Dean had ripped out the walls of the room, and had begun the process of updating the wiring. For the first time in Emma's memory, Dean allowed the girls to use the room as a TV room, even if there were no walls.

Emma was lying on her stomach on the mattress watching an Elvis Presley movie, one where he lived in Hawaii, when Dean walked into the room. Out of the corner of her eye, Emma saw Dean walk toward the back of the room. She assumed he was getting something he needed for the garage. Katie and Amy were just down the hall, so Emma ignored Dean and focused on her movie. On the screen of the TV, Elvis was singing to a pretty girl.

When Emma felt the mattress shift, she turned her head to see what caused it. She saw that Dean was squatting down and that his knee digging in to the edge of the mattress was what was causing the mattress to shift.

Nervously, Emma watched as Dean crawled on his knees toward her, and then stretched out on his back. She pretended she did not notice him and turned back to her movie. Elvis was driving a convertible down a road in Hawaii.

Emma felt a hand run up her leg and rest on her butt. As if she were as light as a piece of paper, Dean flipped her over onto her back. He flipped her over so fast and violently that it knocked the wind out of her.

Dean pinned his thirteen-year-old daughter to the mattress, his knees holding her so she could not escape. As she thrashed about, trying to be free, he reached down and unsnapped her jeans.

When Emma felt and heard the snap on her jeans give way, all reason left her, and not caring if Dean beat her death, she fought for her life. With every bit of strength she had, she kicked and clawed. She clawed at his face.

Straddling her, Dean grabbed Emma's wrists and pressed them against the mattress, pinning her upper body so she could not get away from him. She began kicking her feet, using the strength she did not know she had, to lift and try to kick his back, to get him off her.

Dean rose up on his knees, and before Emma could get away, dug his hands into the waist of her jeans. Getting a firm grip, he pulled so hard that her body was pulled off of the mattress. Emma's shoulders, hips and legs were off the mattress, in the air. As Dean continued to tug at her jeans, Emma writhed and kicked. She caught his chin with one of her feet. When Emma felt her foot make contact with Dean's jaw, she knew she had gone too far in her struggle to keep her jeans on, but she didn't care, and she kept kicking.

She felt the pressure on her waist lesson, and fell to the mattress. For a second, Dean stared down at Emma, then he scooted toward the edge of the bed and climbed to his feet. And as Emma watched, without a backward glance, Dean walked out of the room.

Emma sat up in the middle of the mattress. She couldn't believe what had just happened. Dean had just attacked her, with her sisters in the next room, and she had fought him off her. And she was still alive! He had walked away. Maybe something or someone was looking over her after all, Emma considered. Maybe . . . Jesus.

21

Emma was freezing. She was sitting on her bed, her back pressed against the back of the headboard, her knees pulled to her chest. The warm air drifting up from the room below, through the one vent in the floor, was doing nothing to dispel the winter evening chill. Emma leaned her face on her knee. Her nose touched her hand. Cold—just as it would be if she was outside, but she was not outside. Every winter it was the same thing, it was freezing in her bedroom. The cold was not something she ever got used to, especially in her bedroom.

Christmas break had begun. Christmas was just a few days away. At least this year they had a tree, Emma reflected, a ridiculous looking tree. The tree was standing in the middle of the living room and was shorter than Emma was. Katie, Amy and Emma had decorated the tree, mostly with tinsel. Maureen had taken all of her ornaments with her when she moved out, so Dean had picked up a box of cheap balls from somewhere. Emma hadn't wanted to hurt his feelings by telling him his tree was really lame, but it really was a lame tree.

Dean had placed a few small presents under the tree, more than likely Ruth's idea, since they were dating again. Upon examination of the presents under the tree, Emma noticed that three had her name written on the tags. The boxes were small enough to be jewelry she decided, and the most intriguing wrapped gift was shaped like a tube of Chap Stick.

She had never received jewelry before, and currently did not even own a single piece. The Chap Stick, Emma thought thanklessly, would provide relief from the harsh cold of her bedroom during the winter months. No longer would she suffer the effects of crusty lips during the blustery winter season. Chap Stick, well that gift was probably from Dean, quite the splurge, and a gift from the heart that would just keep on giving. Dean was an avid Chap Stick user, fond of rolling his black tube of Chap Stick over his big fleshy lips. The thought made Emma shudder.

Emma thought it odd that Amy did not have a single gift under the tree, not even the Chap Stick shaped gift. She had a feeling that Dean was jealous of Amy's new boyfriend and was sending her a message. No presents for you, Amy, until you ditch the boy.

When she was a little girl, Emma had loved believing in Santa Claus, and loved the story of the birth of Jesus. However, that had been a long time ago, when Maureen had still lived with them. This year, Emma was lucky to be getting the three presents that were under the tree. Aside from that, it was just going to be another dreary day at the house on Third Street. Last year had been the first Christmas spent without Maureen, her little sister, and her brothers.

Emma knew that Christmas had been Maureen's thing, and that Dean never forked out any of his money, or time, to make the day special. Maureen used to put a lot of thought and effort into the day and the weeks leading up to Santa's arrival. Each of the kids would give her a list of things they wished for, and for the most part, they received their most wanted items, and Christmas dinner was a feast prepared entirely by Maureen. Last year—the first year without her stepmother, and brothers and sister—for Christmas, Dean had handed Emma, Katie and Amy, each sixty dollars cash, instructing them to find their way to a store to purchase clothing, a challenge considering the nearest store was twenty miles away. That evening Dean had surprised his daughters with an uncomfortable dinner at a diner, where they consumed cheeseburgers and cokes. No tree. No gifts. And certainly, no Christmas magic that day.

This Christmas, unknown to Emma, there were already a few Christmas surprises in the works. A few days after Christmas, Emma, Katie and Amy were given a grand surprise when Dean announced that their mother, Nancy, was coming to visit. Emma had thought her real mother was dead, and did not remember her because she had left when Emma very young.

The next afternoon, Katie, Amy, and Emma waited for their mother to arrive at their home to get a look at the children she had abandoned. Katie, Amy and Emma had changed into their very best borrowed clothes that afternoon so they could impress their long lost mother with how pretty they were. Emma felt like a tall, geeky troll standing inches above her shorter, older sisters, her frame rail thin because of her recent growth spurt. She had borrowed high-waisted, wide-legged jeans, and a short-sleeved blouse from Amy to wear for the occasion, an outfit she knew Amy had borrowed from one of her friends. The jeans hung on Emma's thin frame like a loose fitting skirt. She was grateful for the loaner clothes but knew she looked ridiculous.

Glancing over at Amy and Katie, Emma saw the conflicting emotions swimming in their eyes. They probably think she's coming to save us, Emma speculated, but she did not think that would be the case. Emma suspected it was just going to be another in a long series of unhappy events in her life. She had no false hopes about the visit, no high expectations, instead she just wanted to get the visit over, thinking it odd that her *real* mom would show up after all these years. Emma was not thrilled at the chance to meet the woman who had not wanted her.

How is seeing my biological mother, after eleven years, going to change my life, Emma wondered, bitterly. The last time Emma had seen her mother, Emma had been a baby, just two years old and still in diapers. Oh well, she thought, her sisters were excited to have the woman they did not know, visit. Sometimes Emma felt so much older, and grounded, than Katie and Amy. She watched her sisters as they fidgeted nervously, excited, as they waited for the woman that had given birth to them, and then deserted them. Emma was worried that they were setting themselves up for a very big disappointment.

When there was a knock on the door, Amy, Katie and Emma remained rooted to their spots on the couch in the living room.

Dean walked to the door, and as the girls watched, he pulled the door open. He greeted the people who walked into the living room as if they were long-lost friends.

For the first time in over eleven years, Emma got a good look at her real mother, a complete stranger to her. Curiosity got the best of Emma, and she stared openly at the petite woman who she knew was in her thirties. Hmm, Emma thought, she sure is short and not dressed like most of the moms in town dressed, noting the tight-fitting blue jeans, flannel shirt and cowboy boots. *Where does she think she is, at some dude ranch?* Emma held back a sarcastic snicker. As she looked the woman up and down, taking in every detail of her appearance, Emma decided that she did not look anything like her mother, but she noticed that her sisters did bear a physical resemblance to the woman who was staring at them. Emma felt like a specimen under a magnifying glass as her mother continued to stare in her direction.

Emma's mother had not arrived alone. A tall man, heavy-set woman, two teens and a young girl had arrived with her. Dean introduced the room full of strangers to Katie, Amy and Emma. The man was the girl's uncle, their mother's older brother, Walter, and the woman was their aunt, his wife, Vicki, and their children, Abby, Cody and April. Cody was Emma's age, and was a tall, gangly, blonde-headed boy, and Abby was a blonde-haired, very small sixteen-year-old girl, one year older than Amy was, and a year younger than Katie was. Amy and Abby hit it off right away, becoming fast friends. April was a quiet eight-year-old little girl with thick-lensed glasses.

The girl's mother did not approach them right away, instead she remained standing in the center of the room, and said, "Hello."

Emma was not sure how to respond, and mumbled, "Hello."

Katie and Amy offered a much more enthusiastic and warm, "Hello."

"Merry Christmas!" Walter said, in an overly cheerful voice.

"Merry Christmas, girls," Nancy said.

It seemed to Emma that the woman was uncomfortable, not overly sure of herself. Emma had not spent a great deal of time brooding about her long-lost mother over the years, but as she now examined the woman standing before her, she realized that she *was* curious to know the type of person she was. *Was she funny, kind, smart, quiet like her, loud, or cruel as people had said she was.* So far, Emma noticed, her biological mother seemed quiet, and very unsure of herself, as if at any second she was going to bolt from the house. She seems scared, Emma realized. But scared of what, she wondered, of her three young daughters?

"I have a little something for you," Nancy said, and held up three small wrapped gifts for her daughters to see.

"Come on," Dean said, and gestured to Katie, Amy and Emma to get off the couch and take the gifts.

As Emma held the long object wrapped in shiny white and gold Christmas paper, she watched as her sisters opened their gifts, wrapped in the same paper. After her sisters had ripped the paper from their gift, Emma carefully removed the shiny paper from *her* gift, revealing a jewelry box. Their mother had given each of her daughters a white jewelry box, decorated with a gold-laced pattern. When Emma opened the box, hinged along the side, she found a velvet gold fabric on the inside. She rubbed a finger along the soft fabric of the many small spaces meant to hold pieces of jewelry. Emma closed the box, and felt the weight of the box, a box that her biological mother had picked out for her, her first jewelry box.

Over the next few hours, the children wandered around the house getting to know one another, while the adults sat at the table drinking coffee and talking. Eventually, Dean called the girls into the living room so he could take a few pictures of them with their mother. Posing for pictures with their mother was awkward for the three girls, feeling as if they were on display, their images captured in a Polaroid picture so their mother could remember what they looked like. Like dedicated, dutiful daughters, the three girls stood behind the black chair in the living room as their mother sat in front of them on the chair. Nancy crossed her short legs, and draped her arms causally over the arms of the chair. Dean pointed the camera at the group, and instructed them to smile, which they did, large silly grins that lacked sincerity stretched across their faces.

After the image was captured, Emma stared at the photo, watched it develop, and as the image became more clearly defined, four faces grinned back at her. Odd, Emma thought, anyone looking at this photo, if they did not know the story behind the photo, that her mother had abandoned them when she was a toddler, would think it was a happy picture of a loving mom with her adoring daughters. But Emma knew that it was all fake, as fake as the smiles on their faces, and handed the picture to her mother.

After the photo session, Emma sat on the couch in the living room and watched the adults resume their coffee-drinking, and watched the kids sitting on the floor laughing about a comment that Abby had made. She was struck by how ridiculous the entire visit was. Everyone was pretending it was a typical Sunday gathering. Again, it struck her how nutty her family was, and she wondered, how could she possibly be related to these crazy people!

Emma wished the evening away, wanted her guests to leave so they could all resume their lives, stop pretending their lives were other than they were. She wanted to get back to the book she had been reading earlier in the day. Her head snapped toward the kitchen when she saw a chair push back and her uncle stand up. The rest of the adult group pushed back their chairs, stood up, and then walked into the living room. Thank goodness, Emma thought, relieved that the evening was almost over. *They were finally leaving.*

"How would you girls like to spend part of the break with your mom?" Dean asked as if the idea had just come to him.

Emma was so surprised by the question that she felt as if her eyes were going to pop out of her head. She stared at Dean, and then stared at her mother who had taken on her earlier uncomfortable demeanor. *He has got to be kidding!* Dean wanted her to go off to some strange place with people she did not know. Lately, Dean had all but eliminated her spending the night privileges, and now . . . now it was okay to spend the night . . . with *strangers*! Emma was shocked, and was growing more irritable by the minute.

"Sure," Katie and Amy said, excitedly.

Emma could not believe her sisters were excited to go off to who knew where with these strange people. She listened to Amy and Abby chatter away, excited that the cousins would be joining them on their drive home, wherever that was. In a huff, Emma followed Katie, Amy and Abby up the steps to their bedroom. She needed to pack a sack for the unwelcome adventure.

What other type of crazy could happen, Emma wondered a half an hour later as she climbed into her uncle's old, white and brown station wagon. As the car pulled away from the house, Emma looked out the window and watched the house on Third Street become smaller, and then disappear from view.

They drove for several hours, much of the drive through deserted country roads, and it was late by the time they reached their destination.

"We're here!" Walter shouted. "Here's our castle!" A cartoon character giggle escaped from his weird looking face.

At first, Emma thought her uncle had pulled up in front of a shed or storage building, but as she squinted, and stared at the building in the middle of nowhere, she realized it was a house. It wasn't really a house, but a shack, she thought in dismay as she stood next to the car, and waited for her sisters to join her on the gravel driveway.

Well, Emma thought, maybe it will look better on the inside. She followed behind her cousins and sisters, and climbed the sagging wooden porch. She jumped in surprise when four or five stray cats darted off the porch into the dark depths of the yard.

Emma stepped into a kitchen which was just as disappointingly drab as the outside of the house. She wondered if her sisters were noticing how odd the situation was, that people actually lived in such a rundown house. She noticed that Katie was quiet, too, and was looking around the kitchen.

As Emma followed the group on the tour of the rest of the house, she thought, I'll just keep walking and I am sure it'll get better. She was in for an unpleasant surprise when she walked into a small living room containing a couple of sagging couches, chairs and a Television set. The floor was even worse than the worn furniture, bare plywood floor. There was no carpet, not even cheap torn up linoleum, just bare wood. Emma continued on through a hallway that led to the bathroom, and peering into the bathroom, she noticed that there were no curtains on the bathroom window.

Nice, Emma thought sarcastically. Next, she was led through the hall to a small bedroom, which she was told was her aunt and uncle's room. A small room was off their bedroom where the three kids slept.

It had been a long day for Emma, and finding out that she would be spending the next few days in a dark, dirty shack with people she did not know, had just topped off awkward with a side of she was so over it.

Someone turned on a radio, a very loud radio, and Emma saw her uncle pop open a beer can and let out another cartoon character giggle.

Emma wanted to run and hide somewhere, but there was nowhere to go, so she wiggled in next to Katie who was sitting on one of the couches. It was a tight squeeze because Cody was smooshed next to her, with Amy on the other side of him.

Emma's stomach rolled when she heard her uncle say something about kissing cousins. Nutty, would just *have* to be on both sides of the family, Emma thought, and rolled her eyes. Smoke floated lazily around Emma's head, burning her eyes, and music blared next to her from the small stereo placed on a side table. She had not been at the shack for even an hour and already she was ready to be free of the madhouse. She wanted to go home, home being possibly even less crazy than the shack in the middle of nowhere. When do these people go to bed, Emma wondered, and yawned.

What seemed like hours later, she was shown where she would sleep for the remainder of the night, but sleep did not come easy because of the music that played in the room next to the one she was in, and the loud laughter and shouting as the party continued without her.

Over the next few days, Emma had an opportunity to get to know her biological mother; however, it was a wasted opportunity. The woman in her thirties, with dyed black, short hair, clad in western-wear, spent most of her time at the kitchen table, and focused her energy on smoking packs of cigarettes and consuming pots of black coffee. Emma watched her, and wanted to ask her why she was not dead, as she had been told. She wanted to demand her mother explain where she had been throughout the years, and why she had left her when she was just a baby. But Emma did not ask her anything, she just observed the woman who seemed more stranger to her than ever.

The visit hit a snag when Uncle Walter announced, quite unexpectedly, that Nancy was cutting her visit short, days short. No explanation was provided to the girls. They were just told that their mother was catching a bus back to Missouri. Katie, Amy and Emma were invited to see her off at the bus station.

Katie and Amy were visibly shaken by the announcement, perhaps thinking, Emma considered, that their dear old mom had entered their lives to save them from Dean. In her gut, Emma knew that was exactly what they had thought. She should have known, Emma thought angrily. A woman who just up and leaves her kids when they are babies, could not be counted on.

"Why are you leaving?" Amy asked, tearfully. "Please don't go. Stay longer."

Emma glanced at her mother, and then looked at Katie and Amy. She could not read her mother at all because not a flick of emotion showed on her face, but Katie and Amy were easy to read with the tears and emotions churning across their faces. Their mother did not provide an answer to their question, just looked down at her bag, which was sitting on a kitchen chair.

The disappointment, desperation, and disbelief were etched on Amy and Katie's faces.

It was no coincidence that the girl's mother, Nancy, had shown up out of the blue. A few days before Christmas vacation had begun, Katie had reported to the school nurse at the high school she and Amy attended, that Dean had been sexually abusing her and Amy. She also reported that her stepmother Maureen, her Aunt Marjorie, and Grandmother Harriet knew about the abuse because the children had told them. The school nurse had then contacted the Department of Children and Family Services and an investigation into the allegations had begun. Maureen, Marjorie, and Harriet had been contacted by the Department of Children and Family Services, and questioned about the sexual abuse. They were each asked if they had prior knowledge about the abuse, and they each had lied. They said, no. Dean was also contacted by the Department of Children and Family Services, and questioned about the abuse at his home on Third Street. The visit with the girl's biological mother had been spurred by the investigation, and not a chance visit, as it seemed. Dean needed his daughter's out of the way so that he could focus on getting his tracks covered, which he accomplished with the help of his ex-wife, sister and mother. Three adults stating that the children were liars was all the Department of Children and Family Services needed to hear. They chose to drop the investigation and allow the three Snow children to remain with their father. The visit with her children, proved to be a complication that Nancy was not willing to continue, and knowing that the investigation was over, one morning she asked her brother, Walter, to take her to the bus station. She was ready to head for her home in Missouri. In her opinion, her daughters were old enough to handle Dean on their own, after all, Nancy had met their father when she was about Katie's age and she had managed just fine.

Amy's tears had no impact on her mother, just as Emma knew they would not. Emma watched as her mother lit up a cigarette, her breakfast, Emma thought, and rolled her eyes. Emma examined Nancy for a moment, as it very well could be the last time she ever saw her, her black hair, western style clothing—masculine—and a cruel streak that ran all the way to her soul. Emma's thoughts were interrupted by the sound of her uncle's voice, not his typical silly voice.

"Do yuh wanna go with us to the bus station to drop yer momma off?" Walter asked his three nieces.

"No," Emma said, shortly. She had absolutely no intention of going anywhere with *that* woman *ever*. Her mom could walk all the way through the country, and the next twenty miles, or however many miles it took her to get to the bus stop, for all she cared.

Emma looked over at Katie and Amy, and hoped they would not give the fake-ass, loser of a mom the satisfaction of thinking they cared that she was leaving, by going with them to the bus station.

Teary-eyed, Amy shook her head, yes, indicating that she wanted to go, and Katie agreed that she too, wanted to go to the bus station to see their mom off. Angrily, Emma crossed her arms over her chest and glared at the woman posing as someone's mother, her mother. Emma wanted to scream, *why won't you help? Surely, even a heartless bitch would save us from a madman.* But she did not say a word because speaking out about such things was not done, and if she were to say something, as her sisters had the summer before, the adults would just scream at her, as her Harriet had done.

Stiffly, Emma turned and walked out of the room, the thought hanging over her like a low-hanging cloud, but she *was* her *mother*, that should mean something.

The visit with their aunt and uncle ended earlier than planned. The reason for the visit had been to allow Katie, Amy and Emma to get to know their mother, at least that was what Dean had claimed. Her untimely and unexpected departure back to her real life meant that there was no reason to continue the visit.

Amy was devastated that their mother had abandoned them. Emma was thrilled to be leaving the very uncomfortable, odd home in the country where she listened to her aunt's sleazy sexual comments, and watched her uncle consume surprisingly large amounts of alcohol. Life with Dean was a nightmare, and she found her uncle's home to be just a different flavor of nightmare.

Emma was as happy as she could be—considering she was being returned to the bowels of abuse hell—when Walter pulled the sagging old station wagon in front of the house on Third Street. She flung open the door as soon as he braked, and went into the house, destination, her bedroom. Walter and Vicki stuck around just long enough to have a cup of coffee and have a whispered conversation with Dean, and then they were gone.

Emma rummaged around for a book on the makeshift bookshelf—created from an old dollhouse—and then made herself as comfortable as possible on her old people dying bed, and began reading about a mystery in a town far away from her home. But Emma found that she could not lose herself in the story, could not allow the characters to take her on a journey away from her real life. She was too preoccupied by the visit with her mom and strange newly found relatives.

She stared at the page of her book, not reading the words, instead thinking about her life. It seemed to her that God continually found ways and people to hurt her, such as the last few days. It seemed that God had the perfect opportunity to send in the hero troops. Maybe that had been His plan by having Nancy and Walter show up, to save her sisters and her from Dean the crazy man, but that's not what had happened. It was even worse, now. Emma knew Nancy *knew* what was happening in the house on Third Street, knew what Dean was. She had probably known what he was when she left him all those years ago, left her babies with him and took off. But Nancy hadn't cared then, and didn't care now. Why would a kind, loving God allow all this, Emma wondered as she looked around her bedroom.

22

It was January. School was back in session, and one cold Saturday morning, Emma was snuggled into the corner of the couch watching cartoons as Katie sat at the kitchen table. Occasionally, Emma glanced at her sister, wondering why she was just sitting at the table doing nothing, not even eating. And come to think of it, why was Katie home on a Saturday morning; typically, she was at a friend's house. Emma had found her own get-away-from-the-house options pretty slim these days.

When she heard the telephone ring, Emma looked up. She glanced over at Katie to see if she was going to move from her chair to answer the phone, perhaps expecting a friend to call her. But Katie continued to sit in her chair, unmoving, and unflinching. Again, Emma thought Katie was acting very oddly, and got up to answer the telephone herself. It wasn't as if Katie was doing anything important, Emma thought as she scowled irritably. She could have gotten her lazy butt up and gotten the phone, in Emma's opinion. Sighing loudly to convey her irritation to her sister who was still sitting as if she were a porcelain doll, Emma got off the couch and walked over to the phone. *Move your lazy butt off your chair, Katie, and get the phone because obviously you can see that I am busy.* Emma glared at Katie.

"Hello," Emma mumbled into the hand piece of the phone.

Emma heard Amy's voice, say, "Emma, is our dad home?"

"Dang," Emma swore, irritably. Now, Amy. Emma was trying to relax, as any reasonable person would be doing on a Saturday morning, and crabby crusty Amy and Katie were bugging her.

"Yes, Amy," Emma said, shortly. "He's home."

"Get him. I need to talk to him. Now!" Amy snapped.

"I don't wanna go get him and have him freakin' out at me! He's in a crappy mood, as usual! Where are you?" Emma demanded to know, as if Amy's location was a determining factor for her to fetch Dean.

"Take a chill pill! *GO* get him," Amy insisted.

None too pleased, Emma dropped the handset onto the end table with a clunk. She would have to walk all the way out to the garage which she did *not* want to do, for one because she was enjoying being lazy, and two, she did not want to place herself in Dean's line of fire. The objective was to avoid him, not approach him.

Emma walked through the laundry room, down the steps and into the garage. She saw Dean hunched over a car he was working on. He had the hood of the car open with his head hidden away in the shadows, looking at something.

Emma shuffled her feet on the concrete floor as she walked closer to the car, trying to draw attention to her presence in the garage. With any luck, he would hear her and she could shout the message across the garage.

Dean heard Emma and ducked his head out from under the hood, and straightened, now standing and looking down at her as he wiped his hands on a grease-stained rag.

"Amy's on the phone," Emma said, looking down at the garage floor.

Rubbing the rag between his fingers, Dean stared at Emma, considering her.

There, Emma thought, she had relayed the message, now to get back to her important business, Saturday morning cartoons. Slowly, she turned away and began walking toward the laundry room, not moving too quickly just in case he had a comment to make that she needed to be close enough to hear. That's all she needed was a Saturday morning head beating.

As she walked through the laundry room and then into the kitchen, Emma considered that it sucked that Dean was now following her into the house. *So much for a peaceful Saturday morning.*

Emma was already curled up on the couch, back to her regularly scheduled cartoon when she heard the kitchen door creak open and Dean's heavy work boots pound across the kitchen floor.

She looked up and watched Dean as he sat down at the opposite end of the couch, and listened and watched as he spoke into the handset of the telephone. Katie was still sitting nearby in the kitchen, at the table, and she was watching him, too.

Emma was beginning to get the feeling that something was up, and Katie knew what the up was. Dean was not saying anything. For once, he was doing more listening than talking. Emma knew that was not normal, and she became alarmed. He was listening to what Amy was saying and it must have been mighty important for Dean to just sit hunched over, not saying a word.

Dean put his free hand to his forehead, covering his eyes. He slumped over even more, and all of a sudden looked very old to Emma. A few minutes later, he reached over and quietly, thoughtfully, placed the handset back onto the cradle of the telephone.

Emma began to suspect that the phone call from Amy, and Katie's presence at home on a Saturday morning, without one of her friends with her, was not a coincidence. Katie had a funny look on her face, and it was then Emma knew that she had been expecting Amy to call and she'd bet Katie knew what Amy had said to Dean, too. Something was up and no one had bothered to tell her about it.

Dean rose to his feet, and walked out of the room, walked through the kitchen, back to the garage.

"What's up?" Emma asked Katie.

Emma stared at Katie, as Katie pretended not to have heard her.

"*Katie*," Emma said, raising her voice.

"Oh, stop freakin' out," Katie said quietly as she pushed her chair back and stood up.

"What did Amy say?" Emma asked as Katie walked toward the hall.

"*Kaaaatie!*" Emma called after her oldest sister. Emma stared after her sister who had rounded the corner in the hall and was now walking up the steps to their bedroom.

A half an hour later, Emma watched as the side door opened and Amy walked into the living room. Dean must have been watching for Amy because Emma watched as he walked into the room from the direction of the garage. She sat very still on the couch, wondering what was going on. Dean was not reacting to whatever was going on the way he normally did. No yelling. He was not throwing things around. He was not knocking her head into a wall, so that was a good thing, she thought sarcastically, and relieved.

When Amy saw Dean, she stopped and looked at him as he stood in the center of the room and stared down at her, neither seeming to notice that Emma was sitting on the couch, watching and listening.

Dean said, in a strange, breathless voice, "Yuh know they'll put me away and take you girls away from me and put you in foster homes."

Amy was visibly upset. Her body shook as she shouted, "I told, and I *know* they'll put you away. I hope they do!"

Amy ran out of the living room, down the hall toward the stairs. Emma lost sight of her when she rounded the corner, knowing she was headed to their bedroom. Well, Emma thought in shocked amazement, the secret was officially out. Emma knew that the family secret wasn't just now coming out, that her family had known for what seemed like forever. No one had cared, so what was the deal, now, Emma wondered, not moving from the couch. Just another day in crazy-ville, she thought with a roll of her eyes, and turned back to Scooby Doo on TV.

Dean walked over to the couch and stood in front of Emma, blocking her view of the TV.

"Go upstairs and pack some of your clothes," Dean said.

Pack, pack some clothes, why, and just what clothes did he think she was going to pack, she wondered, bewildered. Emma shot Dean a questioning look, and then unfolded from the couch, walked to the kitchen for a sack, and without a word or backward glance, walked up the steps to her bedroom. Halfway up the staircase, Emma met Amy running down the steps.

"Amy, what happened?" Emma called down after her. When it didn't look as if her sister was going to respond, Emma shouted, *"Amy!"*

Amy pivoted on the bottom step, and looking up at Emma, responded sharply, "What?"

"What's happened?" Emma asked.

"I told a friend about Dean, and she told her mom, *and* I talked to a nurse at school. So I'm leaving. And you have to go somewhere else, too, and so does Katie. The police aren't going to make us stay here with him. He's goin' to jail!" And with that, Amy turned and rushed down the hall, out of Emma's view.

Emma continued to stand on the step, a hand resting on the worn handrail. Where was she going, and where were Katie and Amy going? Were they going to the same place? There was no one to ask because by now, both Katie and Amy had left the house.

Emma turned and walked up the last few steps and walked into her bedroom. She looked around the room, looked at the beds, dressers, windows, and the old doll house which for several years had held the small collection of books Emma and her sisters owned.

Clothes, Emma thought, Dean told her to pack a bag. Well, that should be fast considering she didn't own hardly any of her own clothes. She walked over to the dresser she used and began rummaging through the clothes that Amy had left behind. There were still a few tops and pants that belonged to a friend of Amy's, and she pulled them from the drawer. She paused for a minute, her hand holding the tops in her hand. Amy would be mad if she just took her things without asking, but she was not there to ask. I need to put something in the sack, need something to wear for wherever I'm going, Emma thought, and carried the clothes to the bed.

She paused in between the two beds, knowing that today, Katie would not mind if she wrinkled her bed, because she wasn't sure if she, or any of them, would ever be in their bedroom again to see that she had wrinkled the bed. She turned to the right, the bed closest to the door, Katie and Amy's bed, and placed the very small stack of clothes on the bed. The brown paper sack made a rustling sound when she opened it and propped it on the bed, and then carefully placed the borrowed clothes inside. The sack was half-full, she noticed as she looked inside. Surely, there was something else she could take with her. She walked across the room and rummaged through the dresser again and found a couple pairs of tube socks, and hidden at the very bottom of the drawer, a bra and pair of underwear. Emma was not sure what she was supposed to take, not sure how long she would be gone. *When would she be coming home?*

How quickly life changes, Emma thought. Just an hour ago she had been sitting on the uncomfortable couch in the living room, in as much peace and quiet as was possible in the house on Third Street, watching cartoons. Now she was not sure where she was going or where her sisters had gone, didn't know what was about to happen next.

Dean walked into the room and sat down next to the sack. He looked down at the floor. Carefully, Emma reached for her sack, watching Dean out of the corner of her eye, and rolled the top of the sack over a few times. She tucked the sack under her arm, and looked at Dean, waiting for him to look up and tell her what was next. In a strange way, he seemed like a child, his body the size of a giant compared to Emma's small size, but the way he was sitting slumped over on the bed, he seemed unsure, like a small child.

This was not the typical Dean kind of crazy, Emma realized. She knew for the first time in her life, her dad did not control the situation, and she knew this would be the last time that she would ever be in the bedroom that she shared with her sisters. It would be the last time she saw the bed that belonged to the dead couple, the last time she walked down the old brown creaky stairs and through the old dark hallway, where for so many years she had raced her sisters through the darkness seeking the shelter of the brightly lit bedroom. It was the end of her time at the nightmare in the house on Third Street.

Clutching the paper sack, Emma turned away from the bed and Dean, and walked toward the door. With her foot on the top step, Emma heard Dean behind her, clearing his throat.

"Maureen's waitin' for you in her car. You're gonna stay with her for a while," Dean said.

Emma glanced over her shoulder at Dean, and then she continued down the stairs, her hand gliding over the wide, polished-with-wear handrail. When she reached the bottom step, she allowed her hand to rest on the swirl of the post remembering the first time she had climbed the stairs, the first time, and the many times after, that her hand had touched the smooth wooden surface. The light cutting into the shadows of the hall caught her eye and she looked out the windows of the double door that led to the porch, where she and her sisters had played with neighborhood children on swelteringly hot summer afternoons, years ago.

Clutching her sack tighter, Emma turned the corner, the sound of her shoes on the wooden hall floor the only sound as she walked toward the living room and then continued out the side door of the house toward Maureen's car that was waiting for her.

Emma's throat burned and her heart pounded a crazy beat as she climbed into the car. She did not look back at the house, the house of lost childhoods.

Dean had called Maureen and told her what happened, that the secret was out and they would not be able to contain it, not as they had a month earlier during Christmas break when Katie had told the nurse at the high school. Since returning to school after Christmas break, Amy had reported to the same school nurse that Dean had been sexually abusing her, too. The Department of Children and Family Services had chosen to investigate beyond just questioning Dean, Maureen, Harriet and Marjorie. By now, Dean had explained to Maureen, half the town probably knew what had been going on, what he had been doing to the girls because Amy had told the secret to some of her friends and they had told their parents.

The secret was well beyond containment and damage control and Dean would likely go to prison for sexually abusing his daughters. Dean had been instructed by the Department of Children and Family Services that his daughters could no longer remain in the home with him. He had sent Katie to his mom's house across town. She was going to share a bedroom with Terri, his youngest sister. It was the perfect solution to the Katie problem because Katie and Terri had been friends since they were little girls, that and Harriet could keep an eye on Katie. Harriet would keep an eagle eye on Katie, making sure she did not talk to anyone else about Dean's sexual predator problem. Sexually assaulting his daughters was just the surface of what he had done, and they needed to keep a lid on it, which meant, keeping an eye on who the girls talked to.

Amy was staying with a friend in town, the family that had encouraged her to tell the school nurse. Now Dean needed someone to keep Emma out of the way, and he thought of Maureen. Maureen had agreed to take her in until he could work his way out of the mess he was in with the Department of Children and Family Services. They had gotten Dean out of trouble last time, so surely it would all blow over soon and the girls would be back in their beds before he knew it.

Except for the rumbling of the car, it was quiet on the drive to Maureen's apartment. Maureen and Emma's brothers and sister were living in a small apartment across town from the house on Third Street. It was an area of town where Emma rarely hung out.

The sun had gotten lost behind the dark clouds and a cold wind had kicked up. Emma pulled her jacket tight as she followed Maureen up the sidewalk to the apartment. Emma stared at Maureen's back, and mused, their relationship had ended when Maureen had left Dean, left Katie, Amy and Emma to fend off the crazy man. Stepping inside the dark apartment, into the small living room, Emma felt out of place, uncomfortable.

"Emma, I've got to run out for bit. Grab a sandwich or something if you're hungry and help the kids if they need anything," Maureen said.

Emma's little sister was slumped on a chair watching TV, and her brothers were rolling around on the floor, fighting over a toy.

"Will you be okay while I'm gone?" Maureen asked. "I won't be long."

"Yeah, sure," Emma said, quietly.

Maureen had been gone less than five minutes when the telephone rang.

Emma picked up the receiver and said, "Hello?"

She heard Grandma Harriet's voice, say, "Emma."

Maureen had told Emma that Katie would be staying with Harriet, so Emma wondered why she was calling Maureen.

"Emma," Harriet, repeated.

"Yeah," Emma said.

Harriet said, "Marjorie would like for you to stay with her."

Grandma Harriet was one of the meanest old ladies, or people, for that matter, on the planet that Emma knew, but for some reason, the voice coming through the earpiece of the phone was that of a sweet little old lady. Hmm, Emma thought, skeptically. She was not buying the sweet old lady act. Emma did not want to stay with her aunt. She was no closer to her than she was to her grandmother. They both made her very uncomfortable. Her grandma was a witch, and it wasn't that Marjorie was a witch, there was just something very off about her, Emma reflected.

"Well," Emma said, "my dad told me to stay with Maureen."

"Oh, now," Harriet said in her sickeningly sweet voice, "Marjorie will be so hurt if you don't stay with her."

Silence as Emma considered what to say, and then Harriet continued, "Maureen's not even related to you. Marjorie is your aunt. You want to stay with family, don't you?"

What was she supposed to say to that, Emma wondered, uncomfortably. The old biddy wasn't going to get off her back about Marjorie. But if she left, wouldn't Maureen's feelings be hurt? She sure seemed to want her to stay with Marjorie, Emma reflected. No matter whom she stayed with, she was going to feel like a little gold fish flopping out of water. Emma wished Maureen were there so she could talk to Harriet. It didn't seem to her that she should be making this decision. Emma wished she'd never picked up the phone.

"Okay," Emma mumbled.

Marjorie's house was the last place Emma wanted to go to, well, right behind her grandma's house, but she didn't want to hurt her feelings, or Maureen's feelings. Harriet seemed happy with the news, and continued her fake, sweet little old lady voice, sharing with Emma that Marjorie would be over in an hour to pick her up.

Ten minutes later, Emma heard Maureen open the door to the apartment. Emma followed her to the kitchen.

"Grandma called," Emma said.

"Oh?" Maureen said.

"She said Marjorie wants me to stay with her." Emma looked down at the floor and examined the pattern in the linoleum floor.

"Is that what you want to do?" Maureen asked.

No, Emma thought, that is not what she wanted to do, but she did not say that, instead she forced her lips to curve into a smile.

"I guess so," Emma lied.

On the car ride over to her aunt's house, Emma mused, three homes in one day. Gotta be some kinda record.

23

Over the next few days, Emma found that it was actually okay at her aunt's house. It wasn't as if Emma saw Marjorie very much anyway, because she was never home. When Emma arrived home from school at 3:45, she was nowhere around, which was great because Marjorie made her very uncomfortable. Emma was not really sure what her aunt did with her time, but was not so curious that she asked her. Emma's uncle, Roger, was not around much either. In Emma's opinion, he was the most okay of her relatives, besides her cousins, Deb and Andy.

Emma thought about Maureen, felt guilty that she had left, and wondered if she had hurt her feelings because she had left with her weird aunt. Grandma had said Marjorie would be sad if she didn't stay at her house, but Emma got the feeling that her squeaky-voiced aunt could care less if she stayed with her or not. More than likely, Harriet had concocted the stay with Marjorie, and Marjorie just did what her mom told her to do. At least her aunt had a nice house and there was always plenty of food.

Emma settled into her new home with her aunt, uncle, and cousins. It was in the quiet of her aunt and uncle's home that Emma began the process of living instead of surviving, and realized how horrible her life had been, the beatings, sexual abuse and hunger. Her aunt and uncle did not talk to her, or acknowledge her presence, which was fine by Emma, and they did not shout at her either, nor did they beat her or sexually assault her, and they allowed her to eat the food in the house.

She began to realize that her time spent in the house on Third Street had been, in a strange sort of way, comparable to life on an abandoned island, with little to eat, and little help from the world beyond the island. Emma knew that most people took food and clothes for granted. Most people took the meals they ate for granted, but to her, food had become a luxury, a luxury she hoped never to go without again. Her cousins, Emma thought, had been living it up! They had all kinds of food, food Emma had never even seen before, in their cabinets and in their refrigerator, and they were allowed to eat it, not realizing what a luxury it really was.

Emma began to relax. Now that she was away from Dean, she did not have to be at a constant state of high alert, no longer needing to calculate her visits to the bathroom for when Dean was away from the house, no longer needing to plot her moves about the house to avoid him. And she could sleep without fear of sexual assault. She could sleep.

Smiles replaced frowns and looks of worry on Emma's face, and the type of laughter that comes with being a child, became part of Emma's days. Her cousin Deb, several years older than Emma, spent time with her, shared her books, and even her clothes with her. And she taught Emma about childhood pranks, taught her how to be a kid. Emma pretended she was a regular kid, but she was not just a regular kid.

Amy was still staying with her best friend in town and Emma rarely saw her anymore, and she never saw Katie, either. They were both in high school, and attended a different school from Emma.

The Snow family was the talk of the town. Before Monday morning, it was known that Dean's daughters had been moved from his home, taken from him because his old habit had risen up again, sexually abusing little girls. Her eighth grade teachers and the principal at Emma's junior high were informed that Emma had been removed from her dad's home, and placed with her aunt. Emma did not know exactly what everyone knew about the situation, but needing to be like the others kids in her class, she hoped no one knew all of the circumstances about the family secret, why she had been removed from her dad's house.

Since Emma had gotten her glasses and hearing aid in fifth grade, and Maureen and Dean had divorced, she felt different, in the worst possible way, from the other kids, and when she went through a growth spurt and grew out of her clothes, she *looked* different, too. She knew she looked like a poor kid, one of the kids no one wanted to hang out with. If Emma had heard the stories about her father, about his time as a teen when he sexually abused other little girls, then Emma would have understood why parents in town were really looking at her differently. They had been waiting and watching to see if Dean would strike again, and he had, this time with his own daughters. One afternoon, it was shared with Emma that the secret was no longer a secret. Some of the kids at her junior high had found out what her dad had done.

The bell had just rung, and Emma—the book and notebook for her next class clutched tightly to her chest—hurried down the hall toward her next afternoon class. She was walking alone, which seemed to be how she spent her time at school these days, as the other eighth graders, laughing and chattering away around her, rushed to make it to their class before next bell.

Deep in thought, Emma almost collided into the boy who had stepped in front of her, blocking her path. Emma looked straight into his face, looked down to meet his eyes. He and his family lived a block from Dean's house, and his older sister had babysat for Emma's little sister, years ago. Out of the corner of her eyes, she was aware that the other kids were still rushing to their classes. Her brow furrowed in annoyance, and noting that the boy had no intention of moving, Emma shifted her weight on her right foot, intending to walk around him.

He continued to stand there, not letting her pass, squinting his eyes up at her. Emma paused, noticing that he was staring with a blazing intensity at her. She sighed deep inside wondering, now what.

Continuing to stare at Emma, the boy quickly blurted, in a soft voice, "I know what your dad did to you and your sisters."

Stunned by what he had said, Emma stared down at him, and continued to stare where he had been standing when he hurried away. Emma stood in the now empty hall, stunned by the announcement from her classmate. How could he possibly know the secret, she wondered. Then, she thought, how many other kids in her class knew what her dad had done. Still standing in the middle of the hall, Emma remembered when she had lived with Dean, on Third Street, walking home from school passed the boy's house, just a block from her house. His family lived in a massive two-story, old house. Her heart skipped a beat as a thought occurred to her, what if he told the other kids. What if they *all* knew what had happened in her dad's house, what her dad had done. In that momentary reflection, Emma's day came to an end, knowing that the secret was likely being discussed by the kids in her class. Emma spent the rest of the day wondering who else knew, hoping no one else would walk up to her and announce that they too knew the horrible, vile things that had happened to her sisters and her.

After that day, the short boy never said another word to Emma about the secret, and she wondered why he had walked up to her at all that day, why tell her that he knew what Dean had done. She just hoped he didn't tell anyone else and that no one else knew about the secret, no one in her class, no one at school. She didn't want anyone knowing what had happened, the nasty things Dean did to his daughters. It was too embarrassing. All she could do was hope he wouldn't share the secret with anyone.

Friday night, Emma's aunt told her that the next morning she would be going with Deb to babysit. Emma knew that Deb babysat for a family out in the country some weekends and was happy to go with her, but thought it was odd that her aunt was insisting she go with Deb. She had never gone before, and it was not as if she needed a babysitter herself, so why get her out of bed early on a Saturday morning, Emma mused. Something was up . . . of that, she was certain.

Earlier in the evening, Emma overheard her aunt talking to Deb, had heard her aunt say that the police wanted to serve her with papers for a court hearing against Dean.

Serve me with papers, Emma considered. She didn't understand why they couldn't just serve one of the adults, like her aunt, with the papers, but then, she didn't really understand what was going on because no one was explaining anything to her. She heard whispers in the halls of her aunt's house, and wondered what it all meant. What was going to happen in court, Emma wondered, would she have to be there when court happened. When would it happen, and what happened after it was over?

Early the next morning, Marjorie drove a very sleepy Emma, and her cousin Deb, through the country, on narrow, twisting country roads, destination, babysitting hideaway. During the long car ride, Emma leaned her head against the window and watched the countryside whiz by. Good plan, Emma thought, as mile after mile fell away. No one could possibly find her in the middle of nowhere, even the police.

Finally, a half an hour later, as the morning mist clung to the horizon, Marjorie pulled onto a gravel drive. Emma sat up and looked through the windshield thinking she had never seen such a fancy house before and in a part of the country she had never been to before. As she stepped out of the car, onto the drive, the silence of the country met her. It was as if a thick blanket of mist and quiet surrounded the beautiful, two-story, stone house.

When Emma walked into the house, into the entryway, she tried not to appear as if she had never stepped foot inside such a beautiful home before, which she clearly had not. She could not help but stare up at the high ceiling, the floor to ceiling stone fireplace and massively large open space, rooms absorbing into one another. Through the sheer white curtains, she could see beyond the house, to the fenced in meadow where horses were kept. So this is where Deb spent her Saturday mornings, Emma mused. Wow! Quiet. A beautiful home, away from family, and she was paid to be here. A pretty good deal, Emma reflected.

The heat of late morning burned off the dew and mist of early morning. Deb and Emma had been at the house in the country for several hours, and Emma was beginning to think she had overheard her aunt incorrectly. Maybe she hadn't sent her on the babysitting adventure to hide her away from the police and the serving of papers. Emma began to relax, stopped checking the driveway for approaching cop cars. Even if they were looking for her, Emma considered, her aunt had done a pretty great job picking this hideout. No one would find her here. How would they, she reflected, how would they know Deb babysat on Saturday mornings and even if she was ratted out, how would they know *where* she babysat.

Occasionally, Emma glanced at the clock; the minutes ticking closer to the time when the parents would be home and babysitting would come to an end. She was surprised when she heard the doorbell ring, wondering who could possibly be visiting the house in the middle of nowhere. Deb answered the door as Emma peeked from around the corner in the kitchen. Emma saw two uniformed police officers with shiny silver badges on the chest of their dark uniforms. She heard a dark gravelly voice, and then Deb called her name.

"Emma," Deb called out, her hand holding the heavy wood door open as the officers stood on the porch, visible from where Emma was standing.

Emma's heart thudded in her chest as she walked to the open door, walking closer to the two men in uniform. She looked them over as she approached, at the guns and handcuffs attached to the belts around their waists.

Emma was quiet, nervous as she stood in the doorway, wondering what they wanted and what they would do to her. Were they going to take her away in their car, she worried.

The shorter of the two officers asked Emma if her name was really her name, if she was who she was. As if they didn't know, Emma thought. What other kid, besides Deb, would be at this specific house on Saturday morning. Were they stupid, or did they really not know who she was?

For a second, she considered lying and saying she was someone else, but figured she'd go to jail for lying, her wrists shackled as they shoved her into the back of their car.

"Yeah," Emma said, indicating that she was indeed the Emma Claire Snow that they were looking for.

The officer thrust a large brown envelope at her. Stiffly, Emma extended her arm, robotically opened her hand and accepted the very official and grown-up looking package from the man in uniform with the shiny badge.

That was it, Emma thought as she watched the two officers turn away from her and walk toward their squad car. She noted the lights on the top of the car, thankful they were not lit up at that moment. So, Emma thought as she rubbed a sweaty palm on the leg of her jeans, she had just been served. They sure were in a hurry to do it, she thought. Perhaps, she considered, as she closed the door, they had other children that needed serving before their day was done.

Later, during the drive to her aunt's house, Emma mulled over how the police had found her at the house in the country. Logically, there was no way they would have known she was there . . . unless her aunt had clued them in. Emma had thought Marjorie wanted her to babysit with Deb that morning so the police could not find her, but, she wondered, maybe she had it all wrong. Maybe Marjorie was okay if they found her, just not at *her* house. Marjorie had to have been the one who told the police where she was. It was all so confusing, the court stuff that the adults were hiding from her. But, as she had seen today, the police and court would find her no matter where Dean's family hid her.

24

Emma had become comfortable at her aunt's house, feeling as if it were now her home. For the first time in her memory, Emma was not afraid all the time. She had clothes to wear to school, food for breakfast and supper, and no one yelled at her, not her cousins, her aunt, nor her uncle.

Her life had become quiet, and now when she read a book, it was not to escape her surroundings, it was because she enjoyed it. Emma felt at peace, her stomach no longer hurt and she did not have headaches caused by blows to her head, anymore. The only time her stomach hurt now, was on court days.

Emma wanted to forget about all of the bad things that had happened, and she did not want anyone else to know about it. But each time she had to go to court, it brought back the old feelings and memories of her life on Third Street with Dean. She could not wait until her last day of court was over.

"Mrs. Fern," the intercom blared. "Could you please send Emma to the office? Her aunt is here to pick her up."

Emma's face burned with embarrassment. She wanted to crawl under her desk, away from the prying eyes of her classmates.

"Emma, get your things as you will be gone for the rest of the afternoon. Go straight to the office. Your aunt is waiting for you," the teacher said.

Rolling her eyes, Emma thought, you loon of a teacher, I am not completely deaf. I, and the rest of this floor of the school heard the intercom blaring. Couldn't miss it, thanks so much! Why were teachers so stupid, Emma wondered angrily. *Good thing the dippy teacher repeated the announcement, as I clearly didn't hear the secretary shrieking over the intercom the first time!* Emma sighed. The office could have just snuck a note into her, real quiet and inconspicuous and could have avoided the total disruption of the entire class. Avoiding eye contact, Emma could see that every one of the kids in class had their head turned and were looking in her direction.

All morning, Emma had dreaded her aunt's arrival, and had just gone through the motions of all her classes, and this, this fiasco, was so much worse than she could have imagined. Adults were so retarded, she thought.

Emma tried to shake herself out of the embarrassment and fear that had found its way into the pit of her stomach and had her heart racing. Fear seemed to be her one constant companion in her life. It was hard to shake it off. Feeling a little shaky, Emma stood up from her chair and walked stiffly toward the door leading to the hall. She heard the students left behind in the classroom whispering and snickering. Her mouth had become amazingly dry. She couldn't suck up any spit to moisten her tongue to lick her cracked lips. Emma stopped at the water fountain and gulped down a few mouthfuls of water, trying to calm her mind before going to the office to meet her aunt. She was stalling, but she knew she had a limited stall time. Eventually, she knew she'd have to show up or they would send out a search party for her. Either that or she knew an announcement would be made over the entire school intercom to, *Please send Emma to the office as her aunt is here to collect her.* Then the *entire* school would know Marjorie had arrived to take her away!

One more day, Emma thought. She could do this. How bad could it be?

Emma's feet slowed, no longer hurrying to the principal's office as she wondered—*how bad could it be—really*. Life had been pretty bad so far, but she knew things were looking up. She began to daydream away from the shiny wooden halls of the junior high, thinking of the events that had transpired in her short life, things that had led her to her days in court. Emma's life had always been crazy, filled with the loud sharp noises of shouting, pain from punches, beatings and the degradation of the—touching. It was the way things were. It was the way she knew life shouldn't be, but the way it was in her family. Life had always been this way, for as long as she could remember.

25

Emma was standing in the cold courtroom, wedged between her two older sisters. She didn't know what she was so afraid of. She knew the judge would protect them. He would never send them back to Dean, not after all of the horrible things he had done to them. It was just a matter of where the judge would place them and how long the judge would make Dean stay in prison. Emma hoped for a very long time.

Emma did not see any changes in her near future, aside from having a dad in prison. After court, she'd go home with her aunt. As the attorneys talked to the judge, Emma looked over at her aunt who was sitting next to her grandma, behind her dad near the front of the room, off to her right. Marjorie reminded Emma of Edith Bunker, and not in a nice dingy kind of way. Mentally, Emma thought her aunt was out there on her own little planet, probably because of *her* crummy childhood spent with Dean. Emma had heard the stories, that Dean had gotten her pregnant when she was just a kid and grandma had lied to everyone in town saying the baby had been hers. Emma didn't know which story was true, but even if Dean hadn't gotten Marjorie pregnant when she was a young teen, having people in town say she'd had a baby with her brother would mess her up. But why would anyone say something like that, Emma mused. What would possess anyone to say such sick things if it wasn't true, and if true . . . Well, her aunt sure seemed screwed up to her, but not screwed up in the same way Dean was screwed up.

As Harriet leaned over and whispered something to Marjorie, Emma thought about Katie, where she was going to live after the judge put Dean in jail. She assumed she would probably continue to live at their grandma's house. Katie had always been good friends with their aunt Terri, Dean and Marjorie's little sister. She was the same age as Katie. It seemed likely that Katie would continue to stay with them.

Terri was grandma's pre-menopause accident child born when grandma was 46. Emma tried to imagine what Terri's life had been like with her mean, old grandma as a mother. Terri's childhood must have been very unpleasant, Emma thought as her face contorted into a frown. Grandma was not one of those kindly old ladies portrayed on TV, baking cookies and stuff. She was a scary, mean lady.

Amy, Emma speculated, would most likely move into their aunt's house. It would be weird, Emma thought, not living with both her sisters, but it wouldn't be so bad, she supposed. Amy would probably share a bedroom with Deb, Emma thought. She wished she could swap roomies, Emma considered, move out of her older cousin's room and move in with Deb. Katie would be graduating high school next year so she'd be on her own, anyway. It wasn't as if they were going to live in different towns. For now, if Emma wanted to see Katie, she could ride her bike across town to Harriet's house to see her.

March would be here soon, spring, which meant Emma could put the horrible winter and court behind her, and it was her birthday month. She had already made plans to hang out with Deb on her birthday, planned to make a cake for her special day. Emma hadn't had a birthday cake in a few years, not since Maureen had left Dean.

Just one more day to get through, one more day of court, one more miserably embarrassing day. This afternoon, the judge would announce Dean's sentence, his punishment for rape, sexual assault, battery and neglect.

Emma shivered because it was cold in the courtroom and because she was nervous. She clasped her hands tightly together. She could not wait until it was all over and she never had to set her size six feet in a courthouse again. Marjorie would never have to come to her junior high school in the middle of the afternoon to take her out of math class again, and kids Emma had known since Kindergarten would no longer snicker at her as she walked away.

The sound of the judge's voice drew Emma out of her thoughts, back to the small cold courtroom; she focused on what the judge was saying as she shivered in the chill of the room. Emma's head was spinning with fear. She was afraid she would pass out, or at the very least, vomit her lunch all over the brown wooden floor. That would be disgusting, she reflected with a frown. They'd probably have to call a recess so they could clean it up. Then it would stink, as it did at school when someone puked and the janitor sprinkled that blue smelly stuff on it and left the pile for everyone to see.

Emma looked at Dean who was sitting at the front of the room at a small table with his attorney next to him. Dean had watched his daughters as they walked to the front of the room. Now he was looking straight ahead in front where the judge was seated high up on his large black chair. Marjorie and Harriet looked stern and angry and Emma didn't get the impression they were angry with Dean. They were angry at her sisters for telling the nurse at school what he had done, angry that they were in court. Emma knew they had known about the secret for several years and no one was supposed to tell.

The memory of the day Maureen was told about the secret, that Dean was a child sexual predator, was imprinted on Emma's mind forever. She had watched Harriet and Marjorie, and even Dean, convince Maureen to keep the secret hidden away. Several years had passed since that miserable day and many hours had been consumed in retrospection about Maureen and the other women's involvement in the situation. Watching Maureen cry that day, sobbing and shouting, had made Emma feel as if she had been punched. Her stomach burned, and her heart ached for all Dean's victims. At that moment, the moment that Maureen found out about the secret, Emma knew something died within her. She had seen it in her eyes. Emma could still remember the sound of Maureen's voice when she screamed at Dean. *Tell me! Tell me what you have done. Tell me—tell me if it's true! Have you been having sex with Amy?"*

Dean had killed a wonderful part of Maureen, just as he had tried to kill the childhoods of Katie, Amy and Emma. That day, Amy had looked as if her very soul had been sucked out of her. She looked grey. Emma had never seen her sister so sickly pale, her eyes glassy, empty.

For hours, Harriet and Marjorie had talked to Maureen, insisting that it was not true, that Dean was not a sicko that raped and assaulted little girls. Emma had sat on the couch in the living room, listened, and watched her grandma, the head of the family, orchestrate her son's future, and his three oldest daughter's futures. Her daughter, Marjorie, supported all that Harriet said. Maureen was a pawn in their hands, and at first protested loudly. She shouted that she thought he was guilty. She believed the horrible truth. But as Harriet had told her, *she was a damn idiot if she believed any of his girls, and if she told anyone else about it, they would lock her up saying she was crazy. Grown men just didn't do those things.*

Emma knew Maureen had not believed them that day, and less than a year later, she moved out of the house and divorced Dean. She had left her with the sicko. The adults in Emma's life were a constant disappointment, failing to keep her safe. But today was a new day. Today the judge was going to get it right and sentence Dean for all he had done. Emma would finally be safe from her dad.

A shadow passed in front of Emma and she moved her head to the side so she could still see the people in the courtroom. Brown, fuzzy color flashed in front of her face. The fuzzy brown was the suit of an attorney that was moving in front of her, her attorney. The attorney leaned down in front of Katie, Amy and Emma.

"When the judge asks you, just say, yes," the attorney said.

Emma glanced at her sisters who were staring at their attorney. Say yes, Emma thought, and felt her heart beat faster. Yes, was not the correct response, not at all. The three girls were silent, continuing to stare at their attorney.

"Just say yes," the attorney repeated. "The judge is going to ask you two questions. Say, yes. And then say yes, again."

Yes, Emma thought, just who is this attorney working for? Dean or us! Emma attempted to look around the attorney to see what was going on in the courtroom, to see what Dean and his attorney were doing, and her aunt, grandma and the judge.

Quickly, the attorney stepped to the side, Emma's view of the room and the judge no longer obstructed.

The judge, high up on his throne, said something.

Emma did not hear what he had said. She glanced at Katie, and then at Amy. Amy looked like she was going to cry, and Katie looked angry.

"Yes," Katie and Amy said, softly.

Emma heard the judge's voice again.

"Yes," her sisters said.

"Yes," Emma whispered, not understanding what was happening. She wanted to demand that Katie tell her what was happening, but their attorney stepped in front of them again.

The attorney raised a hand as if shooing a dog, and said, "Come on, let's go."

That was it? Was it over? Something went wrong. Emma glanced over her shoulder as she was led from the room. Dean was still sitting in his seat, looking in the direction of the judge, not being escorted out of the room like she was, not being handcuffed.

Frantically, Emma looked around at the other people in the courtroom. So, she thought hysterically, the judge didn't care what Dean had done. *He's just letting him go?* The reality that Dean was not going to go to jail was still sinking in as Emma walked toward the door, away from the judge—the highest hope for justice—who had just sent her the message that it was okay that Dean sexually abused little girls. Not only had the judge sent Emma the message that he did not care what Dean had done, he had also sent Dean that very same message. He had gotten away with what he had done to them and Emma knew he would do it again, to other little girls.

Emma tried to sort it all out, the significance of the judge's statement to her, to Katie and Amy, and to Dean. Finally, they had been standing in a courtroom, in front of the most powerful person that she knew, a judge, and the secret had been shared with him. If the most powerful person did not care, then maybe it wasn't a big deal, Emma thought. She was confused, and angry. It *did* matter, she thought, just not to anyone but Katie, Amy and her. If a judge did not care about something so important, about a man who was sexually abusing them, then what would a judge care about? It was then Emma realized that no one cared and that there was no point in telling any adult anything that happened to her. This was a pretty big deal; the adults had heard, but hadn't cared. The judge had just stated that anyone could do whatever they wanted to her because he did not give a crap.

Emma stepped outside, stepped into the bright February afternoon. Katie and Emma were standing near the concrete stairs leading to the sidewalk and the street. Turning toward the massive door of the building, Emma expected to see Harriet and Marjorie but they were nowhere in sight.

"Emma," the attorney said, "Emma, come on now."

Slowly, Emma turned away from the door and walked toward her attorney, and Katie.

"Emma and Katie," the attorney said, trying to get their attention. "You are both going to a nice foster home in town. Your new foster parent's names are Mr. and Mrs. Stamish. Your caseworker will drive you to their house."

The attorney paused and stared at Emma, and then said, "Your caseworker will explain the details to you. Good luck, girls!"

What the bloody hell, Emma thought.

"Whaaat. . ." Emma called after the attorney.

"Emma, Emma!" the caseworker said.

Emma turned and acknowledged her caseworkers presence.

"They're a very nice couple and have plenty of room for both of you. You'll be able to stay together and even have your own bedrooms," the caseworker said in an irritatingly fake cheerful tone.

Emma felt as if someone had slapped her and she gasped for air in shock and confusion.

"What?! You are taking us *where*? What about my aunt? I thought I was going back to her house. All of my things are at her house. Can't I go back to her house? Why am I going somewhere else?" Emma argued. With each passing second she became angry, and then angrier at the latest development in her life. "I don't want to go live with people I don't know!"

Ignoring her, the caseworker continued, "Amy's gonna stay at a foster home with a real nice family, here in town. That's her foster mom, Audrey" the caseworker motioned to a woman nearby, "and you and Katie are going back to Atlanta, to your new home."

Snapping her head toward the woman who was apparently Amy's new foster mom, Emma examined her.

"Katie, your grandmother has decided it would be best if you did not stay with her anymore, and Emma, your aunt said something about cost, it's just too expensive to house and feed you."

Stunned, and embarrassed, Emma stared at her caseworker, her mouth hanging open. Was she too expensive, she wondered trying to remember what she had eaten and how much during her entire stay at her aunt's house. A list of food cycled through her mind, egg sandwiches, macaroni and cheese, ice cream—maybe it was the ice cream, she thought. She had eaten too much of her aunt's ice cream. In a crazy panic, Emma tried to understand why her aunt was getting rid of her, tried to justify why she did not want her.

Squinting, Emma looked up, and said, "I won't eat so much."

Impatiently, the caseworker looked at Emma, and said, "Come on. Let's get in the car."

"Is she ready?" Audrey asked.

As Emma watched, Amy walked down the steps of the courthouse, away from her. Amy turned, looked up at Emma and waved goodbye.

Emma panicked and wanted to cry out to Amy, *where are you going? Don't go! Don't leave me.* It was all happening so damn fast. She didn't understand. What was happening? Amy turned away and continued down the stairs, her foster mom, Audrey, walking next to her. Frantically, Emma snapped her head around, looking for her aunt to see if she had come out of the courthouse yet, but she still didn't see her.

"Come on, Emma," Katie said, quietly. "Let's go."

But Emma didn't want to go anywhere. What about Deb, she thought. Deb would wonder where she was.

Giving in, Emma sighed and followed Katie to their caseworker's car.

She thought that finally their lives were going to be *normal*.

"You girls will like your new family," the caseworker said, absently. "They're a nice Mormon couple, with no kids of their own."

Emma opened the car door and climbed into the back, thinking, whatever, and angrily rolled her eyes.

It was quiet during the twenty-minute car ride back to Atlanta, and much too soon to suit Emma, the car pulled up next to a two-story brick house. The caseworker was right about one thing. It did look like a nice house, Emma thought as she turned her head toward the house to get a better look. She still could not believe, or accept that she was not going back to Marjorie's house. What about all of her clothes and the book that she had borrowed from Deb, Emma wondered. She still could not believe that her aunt did not want her, and what about Amy? How and when would she see her?

26

The caseworker, and Katie and Emma, climbed out of the car and walked up the concrete sidewalk to the pretty house. The door opened before they climbed the first step. An older woman with dark hair appeared.

"Hello," the lady said.

"Hi," Katie and Emma mumbled.

"Good afternoon Mrs. Stamish," the caseworker said. "This is Katie and Emma."

"Come on in," their new foster mother said.

Emma and Katie followed behind the two adults, walked into a very pretty room with large windows covered with gauzy white see-through curtains.

"Girls," the foster mother said, "I want to show you something. Come over here."

Emma looked at the foster mother's face as she shuffled over to her. She was standing in front of a beautiful wooden cabinet with glass on the entire front side, with sparkly glass figurines inside of it.

"Girls," the foster mother said, sternly, "I want you to look at the cabinets in this room. You are never, never to touch these cabinets. Don't touch the handles and don't try to open them. Don't touch the glass. Do you understand?"

"Yes," Emma said, thinking, *how rude. My first few minutes in your home and you are telling me not to touch your precious cabinet and sparkly glass. As if I would have anyway. What a screwed up day! Unbelievable!*

"Okay, girls. Now let me show you where your bedrooms are," the foster mother said, as if she was doing them a tremendous service by allowing them to stay in her house of many sparkly things.

Katie and Emma followed the foster mother as she walked up her fancy staircase.

She stopped at the first bedroom at the top of the stairs. "Katie," the foster mother said, "this will be your room," and she opened the white door.

Nice room Emma thought, except for the creepy door on the other side of the room. The foster mother walked across Katie's bedroom and opened the door showing them what was inside.

"This is the attic space," the foster mother said. "We just store things in here."

Katie and Emma followed their foster mother out of the bedroom and down the hall toward the far end of the house.

"This is my bedroom," the foster mother said, indicating a bedroom on the left side of the hall, "the room I share with Mr. Stamish. And straight ahead, right next to our room, is your room, Emma."

The first thing Emma noticed about her bedroom was the lack of a door. She walked into the room and noted its small size, and the large, comfortable looking bed placed against one wall, and nightstand with a large blue ceramic zodiac ashtray in a position of honor, dead center. Well now, Emma thought sarcastically, what in the world is an ashtray doing in here in my room, a kid's room? Did they seriously think on her first day in their home she'd be in need of a smoke? Perhaps it was an early initiation into the world of foster-hood, she considered. Or, did they assume that because she was a foster kid that meant that she was wild, unruly, and prone to nasty habits? Which she certainly was not, she thought in annoyance, feeling as if her foster parents had just conveyed their opinion of her and other foster kids.

"Girls why don't you make yourselves comfortable in your rooms while I talk to your caseworker for a minute," the foster mother said as she walked out of Emma's bedroom.

Katie walked over to the ashtray and said, in a funny voice, "Gawl, look at this. It's an ashtray! Nice Mormons they are."

Emma had no idea what a Mormon was, had never met one or read about any either.

"What's a Mormon?" Emma asked.

"It's a type of religion," Katie said. "They believe in some Joseph Smith being a prophet or some shit. They have all kinds of rules they're supposed to follow, like they aren't supposed to smoke, drink alcohol or coffee and they sure as shit aren't supposed to have zodiac ashtrays in their house." Katie wrinkled her nose at the ashtray and put it back in place on the table.

"Well, what do they think, that I smoke because I am a foster kid?" Emma asked, her voice as thick as honey with sarcasm. Emma was still trying to shake off the burn of being unwanted again, being thrown into another foster home.

Katie gave Emma one more of her funny looks, and then she walked out of the room and down the hall to her bedroom. Emma watched as Katie's door closed. She was alone, and for a minute just stood in the hall staring at the closed door. Then, Emma turned toward her bedroom with no door to close behind her and sat on the edge of the bed. How fast life could change, she mused. A heaviness pressed down on her as she sat on the edge of the bed. It was quiet in the house, too quiet. If someone whispered in the house, Emma was pretty sure she'd hear them. At her aunt's house, there had always been some sort of noise from someone, or from a TV.

Well, Emma thought, court was over. There would be no more interruptions during school, no more leaving early. Was it really just a few hours ago, that she had been so happy, happy that today would be the last time she'd have to go to court. Happy that Dean was going to prison. Happy to move on with her life. Happy to put her past behind her. But there was a kink in in the moving forward with a happy life. The judge had sent her to a foster home and Dean was not going to prison. He got to go home, Emma reflected. He had sexually assaulted, raped and beaten his daughters and the judge just let him go home, and here she was in a foster prison with the don't-touch-my-sparkly-things warden. What kind of fucked up world was this, Emma stewed.

Right now, her cousin Andy was probably watching something funny on TV, and Deb would be hanging out in her room or downstairs reading a book. Emma wondered when Marjorie would tell her kids that she wasn't coming home. Maybe she had already told them. Would they miss her, she wondered.

The light began to fade in the room as afternoon gave way for evening and Emma continued to sit on the edge of the bed wondering what was to become of her sisters and to her. She jumped when she heard a door slam in the tomb of a house, and then she heard heavy footsteps walking in the foyer. She sat up straighter, and strained her ear, listening to a man's voice.

"Shhh. They'll hear you," Emma heard the foster mother say.

Cue the foster father, Emma thought sarcastically. Doesn't he just sound like a real treat? Emma's mood was becoming increasingly, as Katie would say, pissy. She was in no mood to play the role of the nice sweet little foster girl, after all, where had that gotten her. She felt cold inside, didn't think she could bring herself to pretend anymore. She was bone-weary and climbed up onto her new bed, a bed that wasn't really hers, in a new room that was no more hers than the bed. Aching from sadness, confusion and fear, her thoughts a jumbled heap, she grasped one thought—why. Why was she here, in this specific life, in this body, in this family? Why was this happening to her? Was she cursed, she wondered? Did God hate her? Had she or someone in her family performed some act so abhorrent that God had turned her or his back on her, or worse yet, opened the very gates of Hell on her family? *Why? Why? Why?* She needed an answer.

As tears of despair burned her eyes, Emma lay down, curling onto her side, and pulled her knees toward her chin. She stared at the wall across the room as she tried to find the answer to her question of why. Certainly, no one else was going to bother providing the answer for her. She felt as if her very existence depended upon finding all the pieces of the puzzle and then once found, fitting all the pieces tightly together.

Emma remained where she was, curled on the bed watching the thin line of light on the carpet grow smaller. She began to smell something pleasant. Supper, she thought, and realized she was starving. She had barely touched her lunch.

"Girls," the foster mother yelled up the stairs, "come down stairs. It's time to eat."

Slowly, Emma sat up, and then swung her legs over the side of the bed. She sat there for a few minutes, not sure what to do. She didn't want to walk down to the foster parents by herself. She brushed her fingers across the lumpy bedspread. She was hungry. Apparently, Emma thought, she was always hungry, at least according to dippy Marjorie. She still could not believe that her aunt dumped her because she thought she ate too much. The opinion that Emma ate too much, was that of an overweight woman who weighed her food each night before dinner on a little silver scale in the kitchen as a part of her weight watcher diet. What a mean thing to say, Emma thought and scowled.

I am not fat, she stewed as she walked over to the full-length mirror hanging on the wall by the door to the room. No, she thought, if anything I am a little too thin. She turned sideways and examined her image in the mirror, noting the baggy jeans she was wearing, covering her thin waist and small hips. Nope, just all boobs, she thought and slumped her shoulders. In her opinion, it was a scrawny, long, stringy-haired, ugly girl staring back at her.

"Girls!" the foster mother shouted. "It's time to eat!"

Emma looked down the hall to see if Katie's door to her bedroom was open, looking just in time to see her step through the door into the hall.

"Well, come on," Katie hissed, with her hands planted firmly on her hips. "Let's get this over with. Stop standing there gawking at me like an idiot. Let's go."

27

At least she didn't have to go downstairs to supper by herself, Emma thought as she followed Katie down the curved staircase. As she walked slowly down the stairs, Emma admired the foyer with its lighted cabinets holding sparkly figurines inside. Her new foster parents had a pretty house, Emma acknowledged, much different from Dean's house, and even different from her aunt's house. Emma followed Katie through the kitchen door. They stood beside the small table set for four. The food on the table smelled delicious, and Emma's stomach started to gurgle.

She was getting her first look at her new foster father. He was sitting at the head of the round table, if you could call it the head of the table. Even with a round informal table, her foster father had a mean air of authority. He grunted what Emma took to be a hello. The man had a brown, sun-weathered, mean looking face, and thick, course, blonde hair. Emma noticed a pair of mud crusted brown work boots sitting by the door in the kitchen that led to a porch. He was still wearing his work clothes, jeans and a white t-shirt, and white socks. Apparently, he was not an office worker. Emma didn't know why, but she didn't like white t-shirts on men. It made her very uncomfortable. She wished he would go put a shirt on over his dirt and sweat stained t-shirt. Emma slid onto one of the wooden chairs.

The foster mother said a prayer. Emma peeked at Katie who rolled her eyes in response. It was not a familiar prayer to Emma, not that her family had a habit of praying over supper. Emma wasn't sure how the meal was supposed to go, so she waited for the foster parents to spoon some of the food onto their plates before she fixed a plate for herself. The food was good, and Emma was hungry, not caring if she ate too much, not caring if they got rid of her for being too expensive to keep.

Days passed and Emma became more comfortable in her new home with her new foster parents. There were no more rude exchanges like the one she experienced on her first day. Since the first evening, it had been very quiet and uneventful. Emma got up each morning, ate breakfast, and walked to school, returning each afternoon to do her homework and eat dinner, and then she started the routine all over again the next day.

Emma hadn't talked to Amy since the day of court outside of the courtroom. She had said a quick goodbye as she walked away with her foster mom, Audrey. She missed Amy, a lot, but things weren't as bad as she had thought they would be. At least no one was beating her or trying to rape her, and she got to eat every day. But still, there was any empty spot in Emma's heart, a hollow feeling because Amy was gone. In the evenings, sitting on the couch while she was supposed to be doing her homework, Emma thought about the day in court.

Dean had confessed to a therapist that he had raped and sexually assaulted his daughters, and as a result had spent two weeks in a hospital, in a psych ward. The judge, who had sat in the chair high on his pedestal during her day in court, knew about the confession, so Emma couldn't understand why Dean was not in prison, why instead he roamed the town, just as if nothing had happened. Dean was not held accountable for what he had done. It seemed to Emma that no one cared about what he had done, didn't care about Katie, Amy or her.

Maybe, Emma thought, it wasn't that people didn't care specifically about her sisters and her; they just didn't care what happened to any kid. She did wonder if maybe Harriet knew the judge. How else could Dean have stayed out of jail? He had committed a felony many, many times over. Emma might be a kid, but she knew what a felony was, it was a ticket to prison. Could a judge really take it upon himself to randomly change the laws and punishments for criminals? Could he? Something was not right, but she knew there was nothing she could do about it. She felt as if the legal system had just beaten her, just as Dean had beaten her throughout her entire childhood. Maybe the judge should go to jail, Emma thought, for not protecting kids from sickos. He hadn't put Dean in jail, hadn't protected all of the other little girls Dean would surely harm in the years to come.

Emma had a lot of time to think in the quiet of her bedroom at her new foster parent's home. It was quiet and she was alone much of the time. She realized life at her aunt's house had been a temporary diversion, just a taste of what could have been, for someone other than her. She missed her cousins, Andy and Deb. They had acknowledged her, actually looked at and saw her. Emma thought, after all the years of torment—beatings, and agonizing headaches from the constant blows, the sexual assaults—justice had not been awarded to Emma. It was supposed to be okay. The judge was supposed to make Dean pay.

As Emma lay on her side, curled up tight hugging her knees, she thought of the little girl she had been. Rubbing her hand across her eyes, Emma tried to quell the salty tears that rolled down her cheeks and throat. She swiped the saltiness on her jeans and wiped the palm of her hand across her upper lip and mouth, smearing snot across her face. Angrily, she pulled her shirt up, and rubbed it against her face, wiping away the tears. Was it always to be this way, the pain, and the aloneness?

28

It was a muggy, Friday evening, and Katie and Emma, as had become typical, were home with nothing exciting planned. The foster parents were home too, and it appeared they did not intend to leave the house, either. Nothing much had happened at school that day, except it had been a weirdly warm, breezy day. That meant summer was just around the corner. What does that mean, really anyway, around the corner, Emma wondered. As if one would walk down a sidewalk, take a quick right behind some obscure building and upon pivoting on your toe to the right, just around the corner, the weather or season might be entirely different from what it is now. Just around the corner, well wouldn't that be great if it really happened like that, turn a sharp right and bam, like her life, a new season would occur. Emma had always loved summer, except that it had represented more time at home, no escape from adults during the day.

Emma knew she was in for a quiet night; the doorbell wouldn't ring because it never did. No one ever came by. It didn't appear as if the foster parents had any friends either, as no one ever stopped by the house, except for the paperboy, but he didn't linger around. He quickly threw the paper and on he went.

The foster mother maintained an immaculately clean house, Emma noticed. She had never seen anything out of place in the home, except for the foster father's newspaper. He was a messy newspaper reader, and after dinner he would have pieces of the paper lying about his feet. Of course, the foster mother was ready to retrieve the various parts of the paper when he had completed it in its entirety. The inky paper made its way to the garbage soon after, effectively eliminating any remnants of the reading material lest it clutter the clean house.

After dinner, sure enough, Emma found herself watching what the foster father wanted to watch on TV, the news. As Emma watched, the weatherman made an appearance on the screen, and according to him, a storm was a brewin'. The foster parents, Emma noticed, seemed quite fascinated by the impending event. Emma felt the energy and anticipation in the comfortable TV room. The foster parent's eyeballs were glued to the screen of the TV, not missing a word the weatherman said. The thunderstorm warning had been upgraded to a tornado watch, he shared.

Emma glanced out the window. She wrinkled her brow, skeptical that a tornado was on the way, noting that there wasn't even any wind, not even a mild breeze. The leaves on the trees were completely still in the greenish pink evening sky. It was a wonderfully peaceful evening, no birds were chirping, no dogs barking. It was peaceful.

She was beginning to get annoyed with the frequent, weather related interruptions to her regularly scheduled program. Emma glanced over at Katie who was sitting in an overstuffed comfortable chair in the corner of the room, completely absorbed in one of her *Steven King* books, one Emma hoped to borrow when she had finished it.

Just then, Emma heard a deep rumble of thunder, long and low as if it were far off in the distance. Hmm, she thought, maybe there was something to this storm thing after all. She glanced out the window again and noticed that the green leaves on one of the many old oak trees surrounding the house had begun to flutter. A breeze had just kicked up.

Glancing at Katie, Emma noticed that she was now peeking over the top of her book at the foster parents. Katie, Emma knew, noticed everything that went on around her, and she was watching now. The foster parents looked at each other in a weird what do we do, kind of way. The foster mother seemed nervous as she sat silently perched on the edge of her flowery chair, next to her husband, looking at him as if waiting for something. Legs crossed, the foster father flicked his paper and looked at the foster mother over his reading glasses as the weatherman came back onto the TV screen. Both the foster parents looked toward the TV, listening intently to what was being announced. A tornado had been spotted.

"Where is that?" the foster mother asked, her voice quivering. "Is it close to us?"

The foster father moved a little closer to the foster mother and said, in a low voice, "It's about twenty miles away from us."

Emma looked up quickly to see that Katie had caught every word of the conversation, with what appeared to be great interest. Emma didn't like storms, and thought that perhaps they should be discussing their tornado plan; perhaps get the ol' basement door opened up. Come to think of it, she had no idea where the basement was, she thought in surprise. The basement had not been on the tour when they had arrived at the foster home. She wasn't even sure if the house had one. Surely there was one, she mused. Every house had one.

The foster father placed his newspaper on the floor, leaned forward, and stood up. When he began walking toward the door, the foster mother scurried after him.

"What the heck," Emma mouthed to Katie.

Katie shrugged her shoulders as if to imply it was no big deal.

"We'll be back in a little while," the foster father bellowed from the kitchen. Then Emma heard the door slam shut.

Jumping up from her spot on the couch, Emma bolted to the kitchen door, tearing it open just in time to see the foster parent's car drive down the street. She stood there, stunned, as she stared at the taillights of the car. The leaves on the trees blew, and the wind howled around her. Her hair blew crazily as she slammed the door, and then ran back into the living room.

"They're gone!" Emma yelled. "Katie, they left, they left us here."

"Well, gawl,." Katie said. "With a tornado on its way. They probably took off somewhere safe and left us here ta *die!*" She emphasized the word, die.

The TV began its beeping again, advising all listeners to go to a place of safety as a funnel cloud had been spotted. Emma's anxiety, in seconds, blew into a full-blown panic as half listening to the TV announcer, she shrieked at Katie that they needed to go to the basement.

"It's coming! The tornado is coming!" Emma screamed as the windows rattled and thunder boomed, shaking the house.

Emma's heart was pounding knowing that any moment the house would be sucked into outer space, with them inside of it.

Wild-eyed, Emma stared at Katie, and calmly, Katie looked at her as if her little sister had taken leave of her faculties.

"Well," Katie said slowly, "just where do you think I am going to get a basement. Do you think I can just pull one out of my *ass*? I don't know where one *is* or if they even *have* one. That wasn't part of the tour, remember. And I don't know where our loving foster parents have run off too."

"We have to go somewhere. We can't stay here! We're gonna die!" Emma shrieked.

Emma screamed when the lights flickered and then the room went dark. Thunder boomed as she stumbled across the room toward Katie. A crack of lighting lit up the room. Emma saw that Katie was standing, but not moving fast enough for her.

"Katie!" Emma screamed.

"Shut up!" Katie snapped.

Terrified, Emma clamped her mouth shut. Crack! Another flash of lighting illuminated the room. Thunder boomed. Emma screamed.

When lightening lit up the room, Emma could see that Katie was making progress, moving across the room at what seemed like a snail's pace; destination, the front room, Emma thought. The room lit up and

Emma saw that Katie was headed in the wrong direction, toward the staircase.

"Where are you going?" Emma shouted. She was terrified that Katie intended to leave her alone in the storm, and that she was walking toward all the sparkly things, and windows. Where in the world did she think she was going, Emma wondered. *Has she lost her mind?* She watched as Katie climbed the stairs, walked up toward the second floor of the house, the opposite of what they had learned at school, in every single tornado and storm drill. They were to seek shelter in a basement for criminetly sake, not go to the uppermost part of the house where they'd get sucked out a window!! Emma pictured the top of the house cracking open and blowing away, taking her Katie with it, while she stood at the foot of the steps and watched, helpless.

"Katie!" Emma shrieked, "Get back down here." She was almost in tears as the wind howled louder than any noise she had ever heard before, so loud she doubted that Katie could hear her yelling at her.

Katie disappeared into the darkness at the top of the stairs, and Emma forced her stiff legs to climb up a few of the stairs, unable to force herself to go up the full flight.

With the next crack of lightning, Emma saw Katie walking, not running, down the stairs.

"Hurry up!" Emma yelled. "We need to find somewhere safe to hide!"

"Shut up!" Katie snapped.

"What were you doing up there?" Emma asked, thankful Katie was back downstairs with her.

Katie did not respond, and Emma followed as close as physically possible without actually provoking Katie to smack her as they walked back into the living room. Katie instructed Emma to help her wrestle a couch over onto its side.

"Get under it!" Katie demanded.

Emma squeezed beneath the couch, and closed her eyes as she listened to the wind and thunder. She heard a loud noise and just knew the house was indeed blowing away.

Katie and Emma squatted under the couch as the tornado raged around them. Finally, the wind began to die down. When it was quiet, they ventured out from their hiding place.

Inky darkness met their eyes, lightening no longer serving as nature's nightlight. They stumbled to the front door, curious to know what lay beyond the door. The wind caught Emma's hair and as she tried to brush it out of her eyes, she followed Katie onto the porch. It was still raining. The smell of worms filled the air, and as Emma looked down at the sidewalk, she jumped trying to avoid the hundreds of worms squirming about.

"Oh shit!" Katie swore.

"What?" Emma said.

"The trees," Katie said, "look at all the trees."

Emma walked next to Katie, ignoring the worms as best as she could, and looked toward the direction that Katie was pointing. They stood in the rain and stared at the huge old trees, trees that only hours before had surrounded the house, now all lay split open, insides exposed. The wind or lightening, Emma didn't know which, had caused them to fall. Each one of the trees had miraculously fallen away from the house, saving Emma and Katie. Had any one of the trees fallen on the house, it would have meant severe injury or the death of Katie and Emma.

Emma's head spun at the wonder of it. Something or someone had surely been watching over them. The two girls continued to walk around the house, and more of the same met their eyes, more trees down, and all having fallen away from the house.

By the time they walked around the house, to the kitchen door, bright car lights shown on them from the driveway. The foster parents were home now that the storm was over.

Katie and Emma stood outside and waited for their foster parents to climb out of the car.

"Get in!" their foster father shouted.

Emma looked at Katie, wondering where they could possibly be going. The neighborhood was dark. The tornado had taken out the electricity. Was it safe to venture out into town, Emma wondered.

"Come on," Katie said.

Emma followed her sister to the car and climbed in, wondering where the heck they were going.

As Emma stared out the window of the car, the foster father drove through town, commenting on the damage to various homes, and pointing out the downed power lines.

"You don't want to walk on those lines," the foster father said.

Emma looked down at the wire on the road as her foster father drove carefully around it. Then why the heck are we driving on the road, she wondered and considered that her foster dad was not an overly bright man.

The foster father continued the tornado damage tour, driving, to Emma's surprise, to Third Street. He drove down familiar roads, and then, there it was, the house on Third Street. Emma's foster father pulled his car over to the side of the road, stopping in front Dean's house.

Emma saw a glow of a flashlight near the ditch in front of the house. It was Dean.

"Hey," the foster father called out, and Dean looked toward the car.

Dean, flashlight and a container in his hand, walked toward them. Standing next to the car, Dean leaned down and looked at Emma and Katie who were sitting in the back of the car, staring uncomfortably at him.

"Whatcha got?" the foster father asked.

"Night crawlers," Dean said, and tipped the container so the foster father could look at his catch.

Emma sunk back into her seat and turned her head toward what used to be her neighbor's house, looking away from Dean and his worms, and his house. Why, she wondered irritably, and uncomfortably, had they stopped at the monster's house.

A few weeks later, Emma again found herself wondering why she was being forced to look at Dean's face as she looked across his truck at him. Emma's caseworker had given Dean permission to take her for a few hours for an unsupervised visit, and now she was seated next to the passenger window in his truck, her little brother, Robby, sandwiched between them. Their destination was Dean's favorite restaurant in town, the Country Aire.

Dean, Emma noticed, was pretending there was nothing amiss, as if they had not recently been to court because he was a sexual predator, as if he had not sexually assaulted her and attempted to beat her to death, and as if, for ten years, he had not raped her older sisters. The state of Illinois, Emma thought, was seriously fucked up to allow a child rapist to roam the streets, and even more fucked up to hand her over to him for the afternoon.

29

As the school year passed, Emma felt more and more isolated, alone, as if she were on a desert Island, yet there were people all around her. She thought that with a little time the kids at school would forget all about her new foster kid status. But that had been wishful thinking. Not only did her foster status *not* seem to be fading from their memories, it was if she were wearing a big bold flashing sign on her chest for all to see. *Come one, come all, see the latest attraction, that's right folks, the only foster kid in the entire school*, the sign read. Even the younger kids in junior high—in seventh and sixth grades—pointed at Emma and snickered as they passed by her in the hall. Teachers, the principal and the school secretary were treating Emma differently, too. Before the big family sexual abuse scandal, Emma had been a straight *A* student, and the teachers smiled at her and made nice comments about her work, and even made cute little smiley faces on her papers. The days of cute smiley faces on her papers were over. It seemed that *ward of the court*, or *foster kid* were dirty words! As if they had never seen one before!

It was so weird, just a few months ago, Emma had been the skinny little book worm with a best friend, equally bookish, constantly winning any competition relating to English class. The teacher would call out a word, and all the kids in class would scramble to find the word in the dictionary. Emma was often the winner, her prize, taking her place at the front of the line for lunch. Those had been the golden days. But the days of her speed-reading were days of the past. At least she *had* been known for something other than foster kid, Emma reflected. Being known as a nerd was okay with Emma. It meant that everyone thought you were smart and one of the *good* girls. You know the kind, the kind that do not smoke cigarettes and do not do *things* with the boys. There were a couple of girls in class that had *bad reputations*. They did those *things* with the boys, things that Emma did not do. Emma had felt sorry for those girls because they didn't really have any friends, and most of the kids would snicker at them, just as they were now doing to her. A funny thing began happening as her notoriety as a foster kid grew, these girls of questionable character began speaking to Emma. At first it was just a, *hey,* said in passing, in the hall. Then the, *hey,* grew, eventually developing into more. These girls began approaching Emma between classes, including her in their club of outcasts.

One afternoon, Emma had made fast time getting to her next class, and seat, and as she sat down, one of those girls popped into the seat right in front of her. Emma had looked up to see what individual might actually be seeking out her company, sitting near the dirty girl, expecting it to be a snobby girl, or a snobby boy, ready to whisper something nasty to her. But it hadn't been, instead it had been another outcast, sitting near her so she would not have to sit alone.

Not long ago, a girl, one of the cheerleaders, had stopped Emma in the hall at school. That day, Emma had been dressed really cute in a navy blue, baby doll top, blue jeans, and sandals. It wasn't often that she felt cute, but that day, she had. She had felt good about herself, and had walked a little taller through the hallway of her junior high. Emma had a little smile on her face and was minding her own business as she walked to her next class, when a seventh grade girl, who Emma had thought was a nice girl. . . but no more!

The cheerleader had walked up to Emma, stood right in front of her so that Emma had to stop, or walk around her. Emma stopped.

In a very clear, loud voice that echoed off the old walls of the school, the girl said to Emma, "Do you stuff?"

Stuff, Emma thought. Stuff what? Then it dawned on her, her boobs. The girl was actually referring to Emma's boobs. Why in heavens name was everyone so obsessed with her boobs, Emma wondered, humiliated by the question. It was not as if they were overly large like some of the girls in Emma's class, not at all. They were just your ordinary, average run of the mill eighth grade girl boobs, but with the way her dad and now this girl went on, you would think they were boobs made of gold or something. Standing in the hall of her school, Emma felt as if someone had just slapped her. She was so embarrassed. If only there was a very large rock nearby that she could slither under. Emma stared the cheerleader girl right in her eyes, and in stony silence, stiffly walked around her without making so much as a peep.

Did she stuff, indeed! She would just have to continue to speculate as Emma had no intention of dignifying her cruel question with a response. Although Emma did now wonder if there were other kids that wondered the same thing. When Emma had gotten dressed that morning, she had no idea that her cute new top would draw so much attention and speculation.

30

Emma, Katie and Amy had begun spending the weekends with their crazy relatives from down south. Katie and Emma had speculated as to why their relatives had found them. They had met them only once, during a visit the previous December when their biological mother had shown up for a visit. She had had her clan in tow. It was as if these people had climbed down from Appalachia. They had shown up one cold winter's day, all dressed in matching coats that Emma guessed the country people wore, speaking in a most peculiar manner, all twangy, and actually making up their own words.

Somehow, these fine folks had found them, again. Katie and Emma agreed that these were not the kindly relatives they masqueraded to be. How had they found out that they were in foster homes, they wondered. They had met them only months ago. They lived hours away, so how did they know, and how did they know whom to contact to arrange a visit with them? And why did they want to visit their long-lost nieces, Emma wondered, suspiciously.

Katie and Emma were about as excited about visiting their newfound southern family as they would be to have all their fingernails ripped out. But they both had agreed that a visit would be worth it so that they could see Amy. Amy had hit it off with cousin Abby during the horrendous December visit, and their southern relatives had contacted

Amy, first, to arrange a visit. Katie and Emma knew that they could not let their sister go to the house of weird relatives, alone. They had to go along and watch over her. Who knew what those people might do to her at their shack in the middle of the country. If something went awry, no one would hear her screams way out there in the outback.

One Friday afternoon after school, *she* was waiting for Katie and Emma in the kitchen at their foster home. Her butt was hanging over the kitchen chair, and it looked as if the chair might collapse under her tremendous weight. It was the aunt from hell, Vicki.

Vicki flashed Emma a grin, her eyes and the sides of her mouth disappearing in the mounds of flesh created by years of overeating. Emma saw the leftover lunch and breakfast crusted on Vicki's enormous billowing mumu top. Could she not see that her top was filthy, Emma wondered. Here we go, Emma thought, let's play pretend to like Aunt Vicki!

Vicki had stopped by Amy's foster home and picked her up first. Emma saw Amy sitting at the kitchen table, too. Emma's mood shot to happy when she saw Amy sitting at the table, laughing and chatting away with her foster mother.

"Hi!" Emma said to Vicki, offering her a smile as fake as the one on Vicki's face. Looking at Amy, Emma genuinely beamed, and grinned.

Emma and Amy ran upstairs, leaving the foster mother, and Vicki creaking on her chair, to chat away. When the girls got to Emma's bedroom, Emma threw a couple of outfits and a book in a sack for the weekend adventure. Katie sauntered into Emma's room as Amy was telling Emma about her new boyfriend, and the fight they had just had. Amy was upset and glad to get away for the weekend.

Emma knew she wouldn't have to wait long for Katie to say something hysterical about Vicki. Katie had been saying for days—in her Katie kind of way—that she didn't want to go back to their relatives *shack*, and that Vicki was a *psycho chick*. Who knew what they were getting into by going, again, to the middle of nowhere with these people. For all anyone would know, their relatives could kill them, and then grind their bodies up in one of those big shiny machines they made hamburger out of at the grocery store. Then they could sell their dead, ground up bodies at a grocery store. Katie was so dramatic, Emma thought, but her humor helped them deal with their screwed up lives. As Emma grinned at Katie, she figured her newest humorous story about a meat grinder, was most likely something she had read in one of her books. But her aunt and uncle were kind of creepy. Emma could picture her aunt and uncle in their dark kitchen, blood staining the floor, with body parts strewn about, and a meat grinder on the table. Emma shivered thinking about it.

As Katie explained, Vicki and Walter were just the type of people to bump someone off, always defrauding the system, and finding creepy ways to make money. Emma was sure they had an ulterior motive in wanting their nieces to visit them; it was not out of the goodness of their twisted, hardened hearts. Money was their motivation. They were after money and the Snow girls were going to be their meal ticket. Who would ever know if they went missing; who would care to go looking for a couple of foster kids? Good riddance is what people would think.

The sisters were all together laughing at their private jokes. It was the happiest Emma had been in a very long time and she wanted it to last forever.

31

During the last few months of eighth grade, Emma lost interest in school, her classmates and the town where she had lived most of her life. Katie, Amy and Emma had been spending the weekends with their aunt and uncle for the past month. Most Friday nights, their aunt, Vicki, drove them to the roller skating rink where they rolled around the rink until closing time.

It was Saturday afternoon, and Katie, Abby, Amy and Emma were hanging out in the living room at the shack.

"Y'all should just stay here," Abby said. "I don't wantcha to leave. I hate it when ya'll leave. It's so much fun havin' you. Just tell that old social work lady y'all wanna live here with me." Abby smiled at her cousins as she tried to convince them to move in.

Emma thought Abby was a sweet girl, and thought the better idea was to take her north with *them*. But she knew that was not a possibility, because soon enough they were going to be homeless.

Emma thought Katie's eyes would pop right out of their sockets when she heard Abby try to convince them to move in with her family. Emma looked around the room that served as the living room as Abby continued her sales pitch about having them live in the sticks with them, just one, big, happy, strange family. Where, Emma wondered, would they sleep? During their weekend visits, they all just slept where ever. That was fine for a weekend visit, but not every night. Even Amy looked skeptical.

Katie and Emma had grown uncomfortable in their foster home, especially now that the foster parent's arguments had become more frequent and louder. Katie said the foster mother had probably gotten fed up with the foster fathers drinking. She thought they were going to get a divorce, another un-Mormon thing for them to do. The foster mother was okay, in Emma's opinion. Aside from the sparkly figurine incident the first day they had arrived at her home, they had gotten along just fine. She had been really nice to Katie and Emma, went out of her way to cook nice meals and cookies for the girls. She seemed as if she genuinely wanted children, but could not have any of her own. Katie and Emma were the fill-in kids she could not have. Finally, the foster mother had children in her home, children who appreciated the things she did for them, and Emma *did* appreciate her. Maybe that is why she was divorcing the foster father, Emma reflected. Since Katie and Emma had moved in, their foster mother had life in her house, and perhaps it made her realize just how empty her life had been before with her cold, mean, drunk husband.

Emma knew that she and Katie were going to be moved out of their foster parent's home. There was already a for 4-sale sign on the neatly landscaped lawn. Their foster parents were getting a divorce, selling their house and both were moving away. That would leave Emma and Katie homeless. Emma was going to miss her comfortable, clean foster home with her very own private bedroom and space. She had finally grown accustomed to the quiet, not so quiet now, when the foster mother asked about her day and offered her delicious freshly baked cookies after school.

Well, Emma thought, perhaps this is good timing. Katie, Amy and Emma knew the goal was to find a way to be together, no matter what, even if it meant living somewhere strange. What concerned Emma most was that she really wasn't sure if she knew just how strange it really was at their aunt and uncle's house. They didn't know them very well. Their relatives were living in a shack in the middle of nowhere. Based on experiences with the other side of their family, their dad's side, Emma knew they should not be too trusting. She should go with her instincts, which right now were screaming do not move in with her aunt and uncle! However, it was the only option presenting itself that would allow them to all live together.

Katie, Amy and Emma talked about what they should do and decided to move into their aunt and uncle's house in the sticks, the shack, as they called it. Besides, their only other option was to move to a different town, probably bigger, to a new school, probably bigger, with kids they didn't know, which wouldn't be so bad, they figured. At least no one would know what had happened to them, why they were now foster kids. They reasoned that if they moved in with their aunt and uncle, they would already know a few people . . . their aunt, uncle, and cousins. Emma guessed it was better than not knowing anyone at all.

32

Emma's aunt called the Department of Children and Family Services, and got the ball rolling. She contacted the office in her county and they arranged a visit to her house to determine what they needed to do to their house to be allowed to have custody of Katie, Amy and Emma. Katie and Emma were skeptical. They thought that there would be no way that the state would allow them to move into the shack. As matter of fact, they were confident that upon an inspection of the shack, the state would likely take away *their* children, and then condemn their *house*, tear it down because it was unfit for human occupancy.

They would have been less surprised if a two-headed monster showed up at their foster parent's home than if the state actually agreed to let them live with their aunt and uncle, in the shack. That was exactly what happened, a two-headed monster did not show up, but the state did agree to allow their aunt and uncle to have custody of them.

They were allowing the girls to move into the shack with the condition that each of the girls had to have their own bed. Emma never thought they would be able to pull it off, after all, how were they going to afford three beds, and where would they put them even if they could come up with the beds. It was unlikely, Emma thought, that they would be able to pull off the small beds miracle, a huge miracle for them.

The next weekend, when the Snow girls arrived at their aunt and uncle's home for their regular visit, Emma noticed that the house looked different, cleaner. The girls were met by another surprise when they walked through the hall toward their aunt and uncle's bedroom. There standing tall and grotesque, in the hall, were four bunk beds that had been homemade. The beds had been placed in the walkway entry to the bathroom. Emma stopped and stared.

Wow, she thought, just wow. They were the *tallest* beds she had ever seen. The top of the beds reached almost to the ceiling.

Her uncle walked into the room, his face beaming with pride over his accomplishment. Emma stared at his face, then at the beds, and thought, hideous, the beds are just hideous, you poor idiot. But she smiled weakly at him as he asked, proud as a little boy, what she thought of his creation.

"Wow," Emma said, "it's really something."

That was enough for him. He took Emma's comment as a compliment and walked away.

Emma was assigned one of the top bunks. She had to climb up onto the dresser to get into the bed. Katie and Amy were the lucky ones as they each were allowed a lower bunk. Katie quickly assessed the situation in the room. She found a spare blanket and hung it up around her bed, attaching it to the bed above effectively blocking out view from anyone walking into or through the room. Amy was able to do the same thing. Abby didn't care. She was used to sleeping exposed to all occupants of the house. Emma did not like the idea that unbeknownst to her in the dark of night, anyone could watch her in her most vulnerable state of unconsciousness.

If there was anything good about the monstrous bed, it was that she was in the nosebleed section, mighty difficult for an unwelcome guest to climb in bed with her. The climb was some tricky feat, and one would have to be desperate to try it. It would be a very determined person that tried to climb that mountain to get at her, she considered.

Plus, there were three other girls in the room. Surely, Emma thought, she would be a last resort for a sexual predator.

The fact that there were no doors to the bedroom bothered Emma. Three doors led to the room, if you could call it a room. The door that you walked through to get to the other room and a third door that led to the bathroom. She still just could not understand how they could call this place where they had stuck the four beds, a bedroom. How in the world were they supposed to sleep in there with people constantly walking through to get to their own room, or to get to the bathroom? The bedroom situation was going to drive her nuts! She wished she could at least hang up a blanket from the ceiling to her mattress, that way she would feel as if she had some privacy.

Aside from the weak attempt they had made at cleaning up the place, there were no big changes in the trashy shack. Emma wondered if now that they were moving in with their aunt and uncle, if they would begin sitting at the kitchen table when they ate meals instead of in the other room where they watched TV. In all the weekends that the Snow girls had stayed with their aunt and uncle, Emma could not recall a single occasion in which they had all sat down and eaten a meal together at their small kitchen table. Maybe it was because they would not all fit in the kitchen together. The kitchen table consisted of a metal table and had three chairs shoved under it. Emma was skeptical that they were going to be able to thrive in her aunt and uncle's home. How was this going to work, she wondered.

Later that evening, as Emma sat in the living room eating her macaroni and cheese—Vicki's specialty—she looked around the room at Katie and Amy, who were sitting on the gold colored couch with plates propped on their TV stands. Abby sat next to Amy, her plate wobbling precariously on her knobby knees and her glass perched on Amy's tray. Cody was sitting next to Katie, his plate in his hand as he shoveled yellow noodles into his mouth, his cup sitting on the floor in front of his feet. Uncle Walter sat in one of the old, high back chairs with his brown

TV tray sitting in front of him, macaroni mounded on his plate, and a can of beer sitting nearby, as always. A can of beer was never far from her uncle's hands, that and the green hat he wore. It was as if they were a part of him.

The furniture in the room, as in the rest of the house, looked as if it had been pulled from the garbage, and Emma had no doubt that was exactly where the furniture had come from. It was obvious which chair was Vicki's favorite. She always sat in the same chair in the living room. She sat in the other high backed gold colored chair, the one that was in really bad shape. The entire right side of her chair was sagging, and every time she approached her chair to sit down, Emma watched wondering if today would be the day the chair collapsed and she crashed in a loud thud to the floor, food flying dizzily about the room as her plate clunked down beside her. Emma watched her now as she squatted over her favorite chair and forced her huge butt down onto the worn cushion as the sides bulged. Much to Emma's amazement, the sides of the chair did not pop off with the force of her immense weight. Perhaps another day, Emma mused.

Vicki rested her plate on her breasts. She scooped the pasta into her mouth, a few noodles escaping and tumbling down onto her filthy top. The remains of earlier meals were matted into the fabric of her top. Emma gagged as she watched Vicki devour her meal. She knew that after Vicki cleaned her second plate of food she would begin picking at the remains stuck to her clothing. She would pick at it, pick at the dry crusted food, eating every speck that she was able to scrape off.

Katie, Abby and Emma had many conversations about the repulsion they felt during Vicki's feeding times. It was the consensus that animals were cleaner and more sanitary than Vicki was. Abby had shared that Vicki had always been that way. No matter where they were, it was always the same, filthy clothes and picking at the food that clung to her clothing later in the day, as if she had saved a snack for later. In numb amazement, Emma scanned the room, in wonder that soon this would be her new home.

The weekend was over and Emma was sitting in her bedroom at her foster parent's home. She was comfortable in their house, but lonely. She was confused. On one hand, she was staying in a nice house, a nice quiet house that was both good, and bad. Gone were Emma's friends; she was isolated from everyone at school, an outcast because she was a foster kid. The kids knew what had happened at the house on Third Street. .

Since her aunt had kicked her out of her house, Emma had begun spending the entire day essentially alone, surrounded by hundreds of other happy kids. Both of her sisters attended high school, miles from the junior high that Emma attended. Emma used to love going to school. It was her escape from her home life, but now she could not wait for the bell to ring at the end of the day. She could not wait to escape all the curious, cruel stares from the kids and teachers, the knowing looks. Emma's foster parents were gone quite a bit, and Katie was home most of the time, but she had made a habit of sequestering herself in her bedroom so Emma might as well have been totally alone in the house.

Her aunt and uncle's house felt very wrong, but at least when she was at their house, she was not alone, far from it. There was always a house full of people, and deafening noise. Not that it really mattered where Emma wanted to live. Somehow, her aunt and uncle had been granted custody of Katie, Amy and Emma. More than likely, it was a welcome solution for the state as Katie and Emma had nowhere else to live once the school year was over. Their foster parents were moving away because they were getting divorced, from what Emma had heard. It was not as if the small town she lived in was teeming with foster homes. Her aunt and uncle's house was a place to stick them. One less case of kids to deal with, Emma considered. It was already decided, the afternoon that Emma graduated from eighth grade, after the ceremony, they were to have their sacks packed and be on their way to live with their relatives down south in the shack.

On graduation day, the sun was shining brightly. It was a beautiful day for a graduation and for graduation parties. Amy had loaned Emma the dress that she should have worn the previous year to *her* eighth grade graduation. It was a beautiful, long dress, made of white fabric, with tiny orange and yellow flowers printed on it. Emma felt like a princess, or at least she knew that there had been a time in her past that she would have felt like a princess in the dress. That time had long passed, when she was four years old living with her foster grandmother.

Standing in front of the full-length mirror at her foster parent's house, Emma looked intently at her reflection. The girl staring back looked like a princess. Emma smiled a small smile. Congratulations, she said to herself as she examined her reflection. *You made it. After this summer, you will be in high school, just like your sisters.*

The weight of loneliness was heavy on Emma's shoulders. She had a very bad feeling about the move to her aunt and uncle's house. Her paper sack was packed, and sitting on her bed. After her graduation ceremony, she would come back to the house, one last time, and change clothes. Immediately after that, they were driving south, to their new home, a foster home, really, just as Marjorie's house had been, since the state was paying her relatives to keep Katie, Amy and her.

Emma knew everyone was waiting for her downstairs, Katie, Amy, and her aunt, but she did not care. Let them wait, she thought as she continued to stare at her reflection in the mirror. Her thoughts wandered. She thought about Dean, Maureen, her two little brothers, and little sister. When she was in elementary school, Emma's family had sat in the audience in the gym at the school as she sang on stage with kids she had known for almost her entire life. After all the classes had a turn to sing, Santa and his elves would show up, running down the center aisle of the gym. *Merry Christmas,* the jolly man dressed up as Santa would shout, and he and his elves would hand out a small sack of goodies to every child that attended the program that evening. This afternoon, Emma reflected, for the very last time, she would walk up on that stage. There would be no more Christmas programs in the winter with her dysfunctional family sitting in the audience waiting for her turn to perform. Never again would she see Santa run down the aisle shouting, *Merry Christmas.*

Emma sighed. They had all pretended their lives were normal. Now, there was no more pretending. Everyone knew that Dean was a sexual predator, knew what had happened in the house on Third Street. She pulled her shoulders back, and looked into her green eyes, and thought, this is the price we have to pay to be together. *Together we can face anything, handle anything.*

It's going to be fine, Emma thought, she just needed to uproot her feet from in front of the mirror, or what had been her mirror for a few months, and get downstairs. She needed to get her graduation over and move on to her new life. Sighing heavily, Emma turned away from the mirror and turned toward the hall. Slowly, she walked down the stairs and into the kitchen where her family was waiting for her.

A few hours later, Emma walked across the stage at her junior high, and as the audience clapped, she extended her hand for her diploma. After the ceremony, Emma said a few quick goodbyes, and then Vicki drove Emma and her sisters toward their new lives far away from the house on Third Street.

Author's Note

Signs of child abuse
When I was a child, it was common knowledge that my dad was abusing me. My extended family, teachers, neighbors, and other members of the community were aware of the abuse. It was not required that I verbally discuss the humiliating and horrific abuse, because my body told the story of abuse. My dad beat me so severely that he left bruises on my body, evidence seen by many. Doctors, hearing specialists and even eye doctors recognized the signs of abuse. Although the signs of abuse were visible, people did not need to see my bruises to know I was being abused. For several decades, it has been shared with me that before my dad began physically abusing me, he had a history of sexually abusing little girls. Yet he was not held accountable, and instead he was allowed to be in the presence of children, which included his own children.

The wives of men who sexually abuse children
When my stepmother confronted my dad, I expected an intervention to occur. Naturally, I expected my stepmother, grandmother and aunt to take a stand for Dean's youngest victims, my sisters and me. That did not happen. Nothing was done to stop him from sexually abusing his three oldest daughters, or physically abusing me.

My stepmother divorced my dad as a result of the sexual abuse. I believe when she left him, a part of her was in denial, that the abuse had happened, and the much larger part, a primal instinct, dictated she leave my dad to protect her own children. When I was a child, women were from a generation where they were just beginning to fight for equality, and even today, the battle continues. Sexual abuse was and continues to be a societal problem, one that happens in families from all socio-economic backgrounds. Another problem for women, whose children are sexually abused, is fear of reprisal from the sexual abuser—who is often the father of her children—if she reports the abuse. Often in cases where sexual abuse and physical abuse occurs, the mother is a victim as well, a victim of domestic violence, as was the case in my home.

The legal process is problematic
The legal process is problematic as well, as it often protects child sexual abusers, and vilifies victims who report sexual abuse and mothers of victims who report the abuse.

Suspicion exists toward false reports. Women, who come forward with claims that their children have been sexually abused, face suspicion that they are lying about the abuse. While rape and sexual abuse of children is not a new problem, but instead an age old crime, there exists in the legal world an attitude that it is not really happening unless of course physical proof is supplied, in the form of DNA evidence or a video of the assault (s). Perhaps it is such an abhorrent crime to many, and a crime that some men in powerful positions are committing, or have committed, that few wish to address the crimes.

Statute of limitations perpetuates child sexual abuse and works in the child sexual abuser's favor. The child sexual abuser knows that if he can manipulate his victims and enlists others to help him silence victims; he will not be held accountable for his actions. For years, their perpetrator emotionally abuses victims, and often their families contribute to the emotional abuse, all in an effort to let the clock run out on prosecution.

Criminals of opportunity
If a judge does not sentence a sexual abuser to prison, then the abuser roams free, and continues to be a danger to society, to his victims, to his children and to his wife or ex-wife. Men who rape and sexually assault children, whether the children are his biological children or other

children, are criminals of opportunity. They seek to victimize as many children as possible. One must never assume that a child sexual predator will choose to assault just one of his children, or one child. The reality is that a predator, given the opportunity will attempt and often succeed in assaulting all children in his care.

When I was a child, for several years after I knew that several people in the community knew about the abuse, my sisters and I were forced to remain with our dad, to make the best of our lives, to survive each day as best as we could. When my sisters reported the abuse to a nurse at school, and to a friend's mother, I thought the judge would sentence my dad to time in prison.

Court proceedings for sexual assault, rape and physical assault is traumatizing for victims. My sisters and I did not have a legal degree, so we did not have a full concept of the legal process, and no one explained what would take place during the legal proceedings of our case. The little that we did know was from what we had learned at school and what we had seen on TV. According to what we knew about criminal cases, such as sexual assault, rape, and physical assault, when a crime was reported, an investigation of the crimes would begin, and then once evidence was collected, a judge would render a sentence for the criminal, who in our case, was our dad.

My sisters and I trusted the judicial process because we had no reason, at the time, not to. To this day, my sisters and I discuss our last day in court, and continue to try to understand why the judge did not sentence our dad to a single day in prison.

Years later, more victims come forward
After I published my first two books, based on my childhood, *The Garbage Bag Girl*, and *Rhodes' Home*, I began receiving messages on Facebook from women who shared with me their own personal abuse encounters from when they were children. Their abuser, they wrote, was my dad. The number of victims that contacted me shocked me; there were so many of us.

Why many survivors wait until they are adults to report childhood sexual abuse

Many wonder why so many victims come forward when they are in their 50's and 60's, instead of immediately after the crime occurs. For the victim of sexual abuse, the crime is always fresh in their mind; never forgotten, however in most cases it takes decades to free oneself from those who have manipulated them into silence, often through some form of fear tactic. By the time a victim is in his or her 50's, many of the people involved in the crimes committed against them have died and the threat of retaliation is gone.

Many victims have been coerced into silence, and deal with the pain of sexual abuse each day on their own. Throughout their life, they try to blend with society by going through the motions of life. They become productive members of society. They work toward careers, have families of their own, and often feel that coming forward would be an embarrassment to the families they have created. They consider that to come forward might jeopardize the lives they have worked hard to build. Then, as they enter their 50's and 60's—now the parents of adult children—they enter the unfinished business stage of their lives. It is time to tie up the unfinished business in their lives. They are now in a safe space emotionally and physically to do so. Finally, they are strong enough, and ready to sort through the abuse that happened to them. No matter one's age, a survivor matters.

Messages victims receive

I learned a great deal by watching how the other victims—my sisters—were treated when they complained about being abused. I learned that complaining about abuse would be met with hysteria, anger, and a mob mentality. The objective and end result was to silence my dad's victims. The horrors of what he did to each of us, were not easily discussed with one another, or with anyone else. It took decades to sort out the depth of what had been done to us, physically and psychologically, and even longer to be able to speak about it.

Reviewing your juvenile case records

Throughout my life, I have thought about the abuse that I survived when I was a little girl. I have sorted through many aspects of those nightmare years and those who chose not to reach out and save me from a sexual predator. I have tried to understand why it all happened. I have tried to understand why no one in the small town of Atlanta, reached out a hand to save me. I tried to understand why the judge did not choose to hold my dad accountable for his crimes committed against children and sentence him to serve time in prison, and in the process protect other children from him. Over the years, as a woman, I grew to realize that to understand my childhood better, I needed to stop asking those who participated in the abuse, and cover up of abuse, and instead I needed to review my juvenile case files, which is what I did. I contacted an office in Illinois and asked for all of my juvenile case files. I received a very thick file in the mail, and I was left with even more questions, questions that only an attorney could answer.

Accountability and answers

Victims and survivors have rights. We have the right to be protected, to be safe, and the right to question processes that failed us.

The legal process failed my sisters and me, and protected a child predator. As an American citizen, I stubbornly believe I have rights, and so I exercised my right to be heard. In January 2015, I contacted the sheriff's office in Atlanta, Illinois, the town where I lived in the house on Third Street, where the crimes my dad committed occurred. I filed a new police report. Then, June of 2015, I contacted the State's Attorney's office in Illinois, and several other offices, requesting information about the statute of limitations in my juvenile case, and also an explanation as to where the break down in the case happened, why he had not been sentenced to serve time in prison.

Of course, I will always have questions that may never be answered, such as why, when I was a ward of the court, did my caseworker allow a confessed child rapist permission to have unsupervised visits with me.

Why did my foster family drive across town and stop to visit with my dad, a confessed child rapist, with me in the car?

Judge's that do not hold child predators accountable for their crimes, allow them to remain free, send a clear and damaging message to both the predator and his victim (s). The message to the victim (s) is that they do not matter and that they should find a way within themselves to minimize the damage done to them. Victims are conditioned into believing that their voice does not count, and that reporting abuse will not end the abuse. Victims take what the judicial system taught them into their adult lives, which is a skewed sense of their value, and a minimization of abuse. If a victim does not seek therapy or sort out and have a healthy view of the childhood abuse, they may be open for future abuse. Abusers are empowered when a judge allows them to remain free, and have the freedom to abuse again.

Families of origin often continue mental abuse well into a victim's adult years

Throughout my life, until I severed ties with most of my family of origin, the older generation, my grandmother, aunt, and stepmother each tried to foster a relationship between my dad and me. This is common in severely dysfunctional families where abuse has occurred, and the child predator is excused by the legal system of his crimes. In my case, since I did not have the benefit of healthy role models in the form of aunts, uncles, or parents in my family of origin, instead I chose to seek therapy to gain a healthy perspective about my past and my family. I also distanced myself in miles and emotion from the heads of my family. I was able to understand the severity of damage caused to me, not only by my family of origin, but also by the social service system and even the judicial system.

Severing ties with past abusers

Abused children often find that the women and men they become is a solitary journey, one where they severe attachments with their dysfunctional members of their family of origin. In the absence of the toxic foundation, they have the freedom and the hard work of planting the seeds of healthy, new beginnings. In the beginning, it is a lonely, solitary journey as the survivor finds few in his or her family that can be part of his or her healthy life. But for future generations, it is the best way, the only way to ensure that the damage of past generations will not carry over to one's own children and grandchildren.

My life, as a woman, writer and survivor
I published my first book, *The Garbage Bag Girl*, in 2012, my second book, *Rhodes' Home*, in 2013, a novel, *Through the Rain*, in 2014, and *The House on Third Street*, in 2015. When I began writing, my goal was to be an example for both at-risk youth and foster parents, of what an ex-foster kid could accomplish. Since those early writing days, my objective has expanded to include sharing the journey of pain, abused children experience, physically and emotionally, and the continued journey. Additionally, I felt it important to share the difficulty a victim and then survivor has in coming forward and reporting abuse, even decades after the abuse occurred, and why they come forward decades after abuse occurs.

Of my four books published thus far, *The House on Third Street* was the most difficult to write. I began performing research for this book in 2000, I just didn't realize at the time. As I wrote the book, I had to force myself to do what I could not do when I was a little girl, I let the feelings wash over me, the memories of the blows to my body, the hands that sexually assaulted me, the fear, the pain, the humiliation and the brokenness.

Life as a published author, like most things in life, has not been what I expected. After writing and publishing my first two books, a reporter from the local paper from my childhood hometown, wrote a piece about my books. I scheduled a couple book-signing events, one in the town I lived in when I was a little girl in Atlanta, Illinois. The publication of my life story created quite the buzz. Surprisingly, just as had happened when I was a child, many attempted to keep the secret that my dad was a child sexual predator from being exposed. I discovered there were those in my family that had erased the crimes, and me. It was shared with family, a new generation that I had never met, will likely never meet, that my dad did not have other children, outside of the family he created after my sisters and I were rescued from him. My sisters and I had been erased, which meant, so had his crimes against children.

The dream

When I was as a child, I envisioned that I would live my life with my two older sisters in a loving home. I had not worked out the details of who this happy family would be. It really had not entered my mind that I would end up in a foster home. I didn't know a single child who lived in a foster home. I had not considered that we might live with a relative once rescued from the house on Third Street. I just knew that one day we would be free.

Children can be very accepting, more accepting of one another than adults are accepting of their peers, but at times, children can be incredibly cruel, especially to children different from themselves, such as foster children, poor children or children with bruises.

My childhood was difficult, a nightmare really, and one would think that once I was saved from my childhood home of abuse, all would be perfect, a land of sunshine, play and childhood. But that was not the case. Children should busy their days with play, trying on characters from the super hero shows they watch, or fairy tale characters from Disney movies. Much of my childhood was spent trying to be the incredible invisible girl to avoid beatings and sexual abuse.

The process of hoping, praying and reporting child abuse, in my case, was typical. Often in cases of child abuse, someone knows about it, a family member, neighbor, family friend, teacher or pastor, but they do not report the abuse. In my case, there were numerous people who knew about the abuse, and throughout my adult years, I have been made aware that there were many more people than I realized that knew about the abuse. It is difficult to be saved from abuse largely because communities turn away from victims because they do not want to get involved.

It took years after the first official report of abuse before action was taken. Over the years, several reports were made to schools, two different schools, and several adults were told about the abuse, outside of the school.

Court

If a case makes it to court, it is seen as a victory for the victims, as if the sky opens up, the sun shines down on them, and doves fly off into the sky. In reality, it is a terrifying experience in which the caseworkers, foster parents, attorneys and judges share nothing of the process with the victim. I, as a minor and one of the victims, had little say in the charges made against the abuser, and no say in the sentence that was rendered. In my case, my biological father confessed to raping his daughters. He had been raping and sexually assaulting his daughters for over 10 years, almost a thousand rapes, and even more sexual assaults. Yet, the attorneys and judge chose to lesson his crimes to neglect.

Society can be unkind to its survivors, causing them further harm because after a child comes forward and reports abuse, they are seen as damaged, whereas all the previous years when they were experiencing abuse, surviving each day, they were just another student, another child. There is a prejudice against survivors once they receive the title, foster child, as if they are less intelligent, rowdy, juvenile delinquents and promiscuous.

The rest of my childhood was spent in different towns, schools and foster homes. Many of the foster homes were abusive just as my childhood home on Third Street had been. But there were many good foster homes, too, homes where I was treated well. The years passed, and eventually, I became a wife, mother and grandmother.

My love of learning and curious nature could not be taken from me as my childhood had been. I enrolled in college, and I earned two degrees—a paralegal degree as well as a psychology degree. I graduated Magna Cum Laude.

I have had a rich career in management, human resources and technology roles. Too often, my work life, just as my childhood was challenging. I worked in the automotive industry in human resources, and in human resources for other companies, and I saw the best and the worst of people. I was able to fight for disability insurance employees deserved, was an ear for employees after loss of loved ones, aide in reentry to work, and investigated sexual harassment and bullying cases. And I even had my own sexual harassment and sexual assault complaints at various companies.

The greatest teacher
My life journey has been my greatest teacher. I have travelled and lived in other countries, and worked for international companies as well as small business owned companies. The result of all that I witnessed and experienced, catapulted me to become a writer and speaker. I share my life experience of courage, resiliency and hope to both adults and children. I have spoken to anti-human trafficking groups, foster parents, adoptive parents, at annual dinners for a children's home, at international women's celebrations, and a place that continues to have a special place in my heart, libraries. I have shared my experiences, my childhood story and my journey being a woman, with crowds of hundreds and even handfuls of people, encouraging those in the audience to share their stories with me.

Each of us has a story to share, and something to learn from one another. At times we must be brave enough to tell our stories, and at other times, we must be the audience for other survivors. We all matter, and all of our dreams should be taken seriously and worked toward. There is no dream too big to dream, or too big to pursue.

About The Author

Carol Knuth grew up in central Illinois farming country. Abandoned by her mother, she lived with her father, a child sexual predator, for many years.

Eventually removed from her father's home, Knuth spent the rest of her childhood in foster care, placed twenty-one times while in the state's care.

As an adult, she lived as a military wife stationed in Oklahoma and Germany. After earning a BS in psychology and a paralegal degree, Knuth spent twenty years in management, human resources, and project management. She then changed careers, becoming a writer and advocate for the victims of abuse. She now acts as a keynote speaker, volunteers at a local women's crisis center and children's home, and works to raise community awareness of human trafficking and family abuse.

The Garbage Bag Girl, *Rhodes' Home*, and *The House on Third Street* are fictionalized accounts of her own experiences.

Also by Carol Knuth

The Garbage Bag Girl
Rhodes' Home
Through the Rain

www.ingramcontent.com/pod-product-compliance
Lightning Source LLC
LaVergne TN
LVHW051550070426
835507LV00021B/2505